Table of Contents

Chapter One
An Introduction to Microsoft SQL Server 2000 1
    Lab 1.1 Search the Internet for Microsoft SQL Server-related Research Materials 2
    Lab 1.2 Install Books Online 4
    Lab 1.3 Search Books Online for the Hardware and Software Requirements for SQL Server 2000 7
    Lab 1.4 Determine if your Current Hardware is SQL Server 2000 Compatible 9

Chapter Two
Installing and Upgrading SQL Server 2000 13
    Lab 2.1 Creating a User Account 14
    Lab 2.2 Installing Microsoft SQL Server 2000 16
    Lab 2.3 Viewing System Changes Made by SQL Server 2000 Installation 22
    Lab 2.4 Installing a Second Instance of Microsoft SQL Server 2000 27
    Lab 2.5 Viewing System Changes Made by Installation of a Second Instance of SQL Server 2000 30
    Lab 2.6 Uninstalling a Second Instance of SQL Server 2000 33
    Lab 2.7 Creating an Unattended Installation File 35
    Lab 2.8 Rebuilding the Registry 38

Chapter Three
Administering and Configuring SQL Server 2000 43
    Lab 3.1 Viewing the Properties of SQL Server Using Enterprise Manager 44
    Lab 3.2 Using the SQL Query Analyzer 46
    Lab 3.3 Using the Sp_configure System Stored Procedure to Alter Configuration Settings 50
    Lab 3.4 Creating a Linked Server Using Enterprise Manager 53
    Lab 3.5 Using the Osql Utility 57
    Lab 3.6 Using the Sqldiag Utility 59

Chapter Four
SQL Server 2000 Database Architecture 63
    Lab 4.1 Exploring System and User Tables using SQL Query Analyzer 64
    Lab 4.2 Exploring System and User-Defined Data Types Using SQL Enterprise Manager 67
    Lab 4.3 Exploring Defaults and Constraints 71
    Lab 4.4 Exploring Indexes 74

Chapter Five
Creating SQL Server 2000 Databases 79
- Lab 5.1 Exploring the System Databases 80
- Lab 5.2 Creating a Database 82
- Lab 5.3 Expanding and Shrinking a Database 87
- Lab 5.4 Changing Database Options; Renaming and Deleting Databases 92
- Lab 5.5 Creating Tables in a Database 98
- Lab 5.6 Creating a Foreign Key Relationship 101

Chapter Six
Optimizing and Troubleshooting Databases 107
- Lab 6.1 Recreating Indexes to Change the Fill Factor 108
- Lab 6.2 Using an Execution Plan to Create Statistics 111
- Lab 6.3 Recompiling Stored Procedures 115
- Lab 6.4 Using SQL Profiler to Monitor Stored Procedures 117

Chapter Seven
Performing Disaster Recovery Operations 121
- Lab 7.1 Setting the Recovery Model for Databases 122
- Lab 7.2 Creating Backup Devices 125
- Lab 7.3 Performing Windows 2000 and Database Backups 128
- Lab 7.4 Recovering the System State and Restoring Databases 134
- Lab 7.5 Performing Integrity Checks on a Database Using DBCC Commands 139
- Lab 7.6 Creating a Database Maintenance Plan 141

Chapter Eight
Security in SQL Server 2000 147
- Lab 8.1 Creating SQL Server 2000 Logins 148
- Lab 8.2 Creating Database Users 155
- Lab 8.3 Creating User-Defined Database Roles 159
- Lab 8.4 Setting Statement and Object Permissions 163
- Lab 8.5 Testing Logins, Users, Roles, and Permissions 168

Chapter Nine
Extracting and Transforming Data with SQL Server 2000 175
- Lab 9.1 Loading Data With BULK INSERT 176
- Lab 9.2 Using the Data Transformation Services 179
- Lab 9.3 Setting up Merge Replication 183
- Lab 9.4 Supporting XML in Microsoft SQL Server 2000 187

Chapter Ten
Automating and Monitoring SQL Server 2000 191
- Lab 10.1 Configuring SQL Server Agent 192
- Lab 10.2 Creating Operators 195
- Lab 10.3 Creating Jobs 198
- Lab 10.4 Creating Alerts 203

Microsoft® SQL Server 2000 Administration Lab Manual

Karen York-Levine

Australia • Canada • Mexico • Singapore • Spain • United Kingdom • United States

Microsoft® SQL Server 2000 Administration Lab Manual

by Karen York-Levine

Contributing Author:
Brian Knight

Managing Editor:
Stephen Solomon

Product Managers:
Laura Hildebrand
Kim Lindros

Technical Editor:
Mathew F. Raftree

Production Editor:
Danielle Power

Developmental Editor:
Dave George

Quality Assurance Manager:
John Bosco

Associate Product Manager:
Tim Gleeson

Editorial Assistant:
Nick Lombardi

Marketing Manager:
Toby Shelton

Text Designer:
GEX Publishing Services

Compositor:
GEX Publishing Services

Cover Design:
Efrat Reis

COPYRIGHT © 2002 Course Technology, a division of Thomson Learning, Inc. Thomson Learning™ is a trademark used herein under license.

Printed in Canada

1 2 3 4 5 6 7 8 9 WC 04 03 02 01

For more information, contact Course Technology, 25 Thomson Place, Boston, Massachusetts, 02210.

Or find us on the World Wide Web at: www.course.com

ALL RIGHTS RESERVED. No part of this work covered by the copyright hereon may be reproduced or used in any form or by any means—graphic, electronic, or mechanical, including photocopying, recording, taping, Web distribution, or information storage and retrieval systems—without the written permission of the publisher.

For permission to use material from this text or product, contact us by
Tel (800) 730-2214
Fax (800) 730-2215
www.thomsonrights.com

Disclaimer
Course Technology reserves the right revise this publication and make changes from time to time in its cor without notice.

ISBN 0-619-12059-2

MICROSOFT® SQL SERVER 2000
ADMINISTRATION LAB MANUAL

INTRODUCTION

The objective of this lab manual is to assist you in preparing for the Microsoft Certification Exam #70-228: *Installing, Configuring, and Administering Microsoft SQL Server 2000 Enterprise Edition* by applying the SQL Server 2000 objectives to relevant lab activities. This text is designed to be used in conjunction with *MCSE Guide to Microsoft SQL Server 2000 Administration* (0-619-03553-6), but it also can be used to supplement any MCSE courseware. Although this manual is written to be used in a classroom lab environment, it also may be used for self-study on a home network.

FEATURES

In order to ensure a successful experience for instructors and students alike, this book includes the following features:

- **Lab Objectives**—Every lab has a brief description and list of learning objectives
- **Materials Required**—Every lab includes information on hardware, software, and other materials you will need to complete the lab
- **Completion Times**—Every lab has an estimated completion time so that you can plan your activities more accurately
- **Activity Sections**—Labs are presented in manageable sections. Where appropriate, additional Activity Background information is provided to illustrate the importance of a particular project.
- **Step-by-Step Instructions**—Steps are provided to enhance technical proficiency
- **Microsoft Windows 2000 Network Infrastructure MCSE Certification Objectives**—For each chapter, the relevant objectives from MCSE Exam #70-228 are listed
- **Review Questions**—Help reinforce concepts presented in the lab

HARDWARE REQUIREMENTS

- A Pentium 166 MHz CPU or higher
- 256 MB of RAM recommended (128 MB minimum)
- A 2 GB hard disk with at least 1 GB of available storage space
- A CD-ROM drive
- A modem and printer (both optional)

SOFTWARE/SETUP REQUIREMENTS

- Access to a Windows 2000 Server, Windows 2000 Advanced Server, or Windows 2000 Datacenter Server system with updated Internet Explorer 5.5
- Internet access
- Access to the Microsoft SQL Server 2000 installation files (Enterprise Edition)
- Access to an installation of SQL Server Books Online

For the most accurate and up-to-date information, see the Web-based errata at *www.lanw.com/books/errata*. E-mail any comments about this book to *errata@lanw.com*, specifying the book title, ISBN, and page number(s).

ABOUT THE AUTHOR

Karen York-Levine is a Microsoft Certified Trainer who brings a wide variety of experiences to her writing. Karen has a bachelor's degree in Computer Science and Mathematics, and was a computer programmer for several years. She also sold computer hardware and software, gaining experience with internal computer components, software packages, and networking. As a Microsoft Certified Trainer, Karen found the perfect marriage of her love of teaching and her technical background. Karen has worked for several Microsoft Certified Technical Education Centers and local community colleges. She now works for her own company, supplying clients with technical training and engineering services. Her technical certifications include Microsoft Certified Trainer, Microsoft Certified Systems Engineer, and others.

ACKNOWLEDGMENTS

I would like to thank my husband Bruce, for his love and support during the writing of this book; for the countless groceries bought, meals prepared, and hours of entertaining the children on too many weekends while I worked at the computer. To my children Benjamin, Emma, and Isabelle (4, 3, and 6 months at the completion of this book), for actually sleeping for the same 90-minute period most afternoons. I also need to thank Project Manager Kim Lindros for all her endless help and patience; and Development Editor Dave George for his keen eye. Lastly, thanks to the technical editors who took every step, and made sure every result is correct.

CHAPTER ONE

An Introduction to Microsoft SQL Server 2000

Labs included in this chapter

- ➤ Lab 1.1 Search the Internet for Microsoft SQL Server-related Research Materials
- ➤ Lab 1.2 Install Books Online
- ➤ Lab 1.3 Search Books Online for the Hardware and Software Requirements for SQL Server 2000
- ➤ Lab 1.4 Determine if your Current Hardware is SQL Server 2000 Compatible

Microsoft MCSE Exam #70-288 Objectives	
Objective	Lab
Installing and Configuring SQL Server 2000	1.2, 1.3, 1.4

Lab 1.1 Search the Internet for Microsoft SQL Server-Related Research Materials

Objectives

The goal of this lab is to become familiar with Microsoft SQL Server and its features, and to introduce methods of finding information online.

Materials Required

This lab will require the following:

- Access to a computer with an Internet connection (Internet Explorer 5.0 or higher is assumed)
- A printer (optional)

Estimated completion time: 15 minutes

Activity

1. Boot your computer and log on, if necessary. (If using Windows 2000, log on by pressing **Ctrl+Alt+Del**. In the Log On to Windows window, type your user name and password in the text boxes, and then press **Enter**. The Windows 2000 desktop appears on your screen.)

2. Start Internet Explorer (click **Start**, point to **Programs**, and then click **Internet Explorer**). This will start your Internet connection. Internet Explorer appears on your desktop.

3. In the Address text box, type **www.microsoft.com/sql**, and then press **Enter**. The Microsoft SQL Server home page appears.

4. Locate and click the **Read the Product Overview** link, or point to **Evaluation** in the left pane and click **Product Overview**. The Product Overview page appears.

5. Read the information.

6. Point to **Evaluation** in the left pane, and then click **Features**. The Features page appears.

7. Read the information, and browse several of the links for more detailed information.

8. If a printer is available, click the **File** menu, and then click **Print**. The Print dialog box opens. Select the appropriate printer, and then click **Print**.

9. To close Internet Explorer, click the **File** menu, and then click **Exit**, or click the **Close** button in the top-right corner of the window.

Lab 1.1 Search the Internet for Microsoft SQL Server-related Research Materials

Review Questions

1. SQL Server Enterprise Edition can use up to _____ processors.
   a. 16
   b. 24
   c. 32
   d. 40

2. What feature within SQL Server 2000 automates routines that extract, transform, and load data from heterogeneous sources?
   a. Indexed Views
   b. Data Transformation Services
   c. Replication
   d. English Query

3. What feature within SQL Server 2000 manages both structured and unstructured data, including searching through Microsoft Office documents?
   a. Full Text Search
   b. Data Mining
   c. Analysis (OLAP) Services
   d. Application Hosting

4. What feature within SQL Server 2000 partitions workload among multiple servers for additional scalability?
   a. English Query
   b. Application Hosting
   c. Indexed Views
   d. Distributed Partitioned Views

5. What feature within SQL Server 2000 enables users to pose questions in English instead of using multidimensional expressions (MDX)?
   a. Clickstream Analysis
   b. English Query
   c. Data Transformation Services
   d. Web Access to Data

4 Chapter 1 An Introduction to Microsoft SQL Server 2000

LAB 1.2 INSTALL BOOKS ONLINE

Objectives

The goal of this lab is to install Books Online, the online help and documentation included with SQL Server 2000, and run it for the first time.

Materials Required

This lab will require the following:

➤ Access to a computer running Windows 2000 (all versions), Windows NT 4.0, Windows Me, Windows 98, or Windows 95

➤ Access to the Microsoft SQL Server 2000 installation files, either on the Web or on the Microsoft SQL Server 2000 installation CD

If you do not have access to a SQL Server 2000 CD, the installation files for the evaluation copy are available from the Microsoft Web site. These files can be downloaded for free or mailed to you on CD for a shipping and handling fee. Be aware, the total file size is large (approximately 325 MB), and the download can take several hours, depending on the speed of your connection. You will find instructions on how to obtain an evaluation copy by visiting the Microsoft home page at *www.microsoft.com*.

Books Online is a Client Tool, and all Client Tools, as well as the server itself, are installed using the executable autorun.exe.

Estimated completion time: **15 minutes**

ACTIVITY

1. Boot your computer and log on, if necessary.

2. Click **Start**, and then click **Run**. The Run dialog box opens.

3. Click **Browse**, and navigate to the directory containing the installation files or the root of the CD. Click the **autorun** program, and then click **Open**. Click **OK** in the Run dialog box. The SQL Server installation routine starts.

4. Click **SQL Server 2000 Components**. The Install Components screen appears.

5. Click **Install Database Server**. The Welcome dialog box opens.

6. Click **Next**. The Computer Name dialog box opens.

7. Select **Local Computer**, and then click **Next**. The Installation Selection dialog box opens.

8. Verify that **Create a new instance of SQL Server, or install Client Tools** is selected, and then click **Next**. The User Information dialog box opens.

9. Enter your name and company name (if necessary) in the text boxes, and then click **Next**. The Software License Agreement dialog box opens.

10. Read the license agreement, and then click **Yes**. The Installation Definition dialog box opens.

11. Select **Client Tools Only**, and then click **Next**. The Select Components dialog box opens.

12. In the Components section, uncheck any checked box except Books Online (so that Books Online is the only box checked, as shown in Figure 1-1), and then click **Next**. The Start Copying Files dialog box opens.

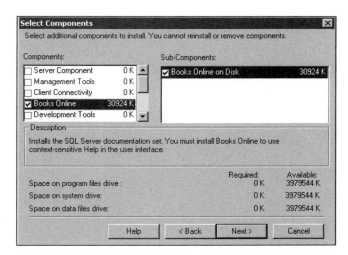

Figure 1-1 Selecting Books Online only in the Select Components dialog box

13. Click **Next**. The Setup Complete dialog box opens.

14. Click **Finish**.

15. Click **Start**, point to **Programs**, point to **Microsoft SQL Server**, and then click **Books Online**. The SQL Server Books Online window appears. Double-click the title bar to maximize the window, if necessary.

16. Click the **Contents** tab.

17. Expand **Getting Started**. This will display the documents and sub-books under this topic.

18. Click **Using SQL Server Books Online**. Read through this information (located to the right of the Contents list, in the Topic pane) on how to use the Books Online tool.

Certification Objectives

Objectives for Microsoft Exam #70-228: Installing, Configuring, and Administering Microsoft SQL Server 2000 Enterprise Edition:

➤ Installing and configuring SQL Server 2000

Review Questions

1. Which Books Online pane window displays the selected topic or the default topic?
   a. Navigation
   b. Topic
   c. Toolbar
   d. Index

2. Which Books Online toolbar button displays the location of a topic in the Navigation pane?
   a. Next
   b. Forward
   c. Home
   d. Locate

3. Many topics in Books Online contain lists of related topics called:
   a. Links
   b. See Also
   c. Contents
   d. Favorites

4. If you use a particular topic in Books Online often, you can add it to your _____ list.
   a. Favorites
   b. Find
   c. Search
   d. Link

5. Which tab in the Navigation pane in Books Online contains a list of index entries?
   a. Contents
   b. Index
   c. Search
   d. Favorites

LAB 1.3 SEARCH BOOKS ONLINE FOR THE HARDWARE AND SOFTWARE REQUIREMENTS FOR SQL SERVER 2000

Objectives

The goal of this lab is to obtain the minimum system requirements for installing SQL Server 2000 by using Books Online. Be sure to record the information, as you will need to access it in later lab exercises.

Materials Required

This lab will require the following:

➤ Access to a computer running Windows 2000 (all versions), Windows NT 4.0, Windows Me, or Windows 95/98

➤ Access to an installation of SQL Server Books Online (completed in Lab 1.2)

➤ A printer (optional)

Estimated completion time: **15 minutes**

ACTIVITY

1. Boot your computer and log on, if necessary.

2. Click **Start**, point to **Programs**, point to **Microsoft SQL Server**, and then click **Books Online**. The SQL Server Books Online window appears.

3. Click the **Search** tab.

4. Enter **hardware requirements** in the Type in the word(s) to search for text box, and then click **List Topics**.

5. Select the topic **Hardware and Software Requirements for Installing SQL Server 2000**, and then click **Display**. The requirements are displayed in the Topic pane, as shown in Figure 1-2.

6. Right-click in the Topic pane (on the right side of your screen), and then click **Refresh** from the shortcut menu. This will eliminate the highlighting done by the search engine, and allow for easier reading of the text.

7. Read through the information that is displayed.

8. If a printer is available, right-click in the Topic pane and click **Print** from the shortcut menu. The Print dialog box opens. Select the appropriate printer and click **Print**.

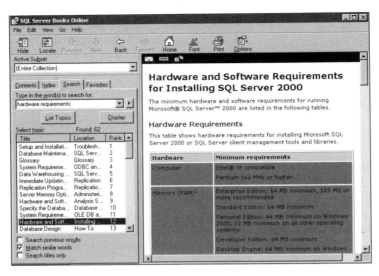

Figure 1-2 Using SQL Server Books Online

9. If a printer is not available, write down the minimum hardware and software requirements for the Enterprise Edition.

10. To close Books Online, click **File**, and then click **Exit**, or click the **Close** button in the top-right corner of the window.

Certification Objectives

Objectives for Microsoft Exam #70-228: Installing, Configuring, and Administering Microsoft SQL Server 2000 Enterprise Edition:

➤ Installing and configuring SQL Server 2000

Review Questions

1. What is the minimum amount of memory required by SQL Server Enterprise Edition?
    a. 32 MB
    b. 64 MB
    c. 96 MB
    d. 128 MB

2. How much hard disk space is typically required to install the SQL Server database components?
    a. 150 MB
    b. 200 MB
    c. 250 MB
    d. 300 MB

Lab 1.4 Determine if your Current Hardware is SQL Server 2000 Compatible

3. What operating system is required for SQL Server Enterprise Edition so that all features are available?
   a. Windows 2000 Server (any version)
   b. Any Windows operating system
   c. Windows 2000 Advanced Server only
   d. Windows 2000 Datacenter Server only

4. SQL Server 2000 is not supported on what type of Windows NT server?
   a. DHCP server
   b. DNS server
   c. Terminal Server
   d. Domain controller

5. What version of Internet Explorer is required?
   a. 2.0
   b. 3.0
   c. 4.0
   d. 5.0

LAB 1.4 DETERMINE IF YOUR CURRENT HARDWARE IS SQL SERVER 2000 COMPATIBLE

Objectives

The goal of this lab is to determine if your current hardware meets the minimum requirements to install SQL Server 2000.

Materials Required

This lab will require the following:

➤ Access to a computer running Windows 2000 Server, Windows 2000 Advanced Server, or Windows 2000 Datacenter Server

➤ The Hardware and Software Requirements for Installing SQL Server 2000 list (obtained in Lab 1.3)

Estimated completion time: **15 minutes**

ACTIVITY

1. Boot your computer and log on, if necessary.

2. Click **Start**, point to **Programs**, point to **Administrative Tools**, and click **Computer Management**. The Computer Management window appears.

Chapter 1 An Introduction to Microsoft SQL Server 2000

3. In the left pane, expand **System Information**.
4. Click **System Summary** to display the summary information in the right pane, as shown in Figure 1-3.

Your system information may vary from the values displayed in Figure 1-3.

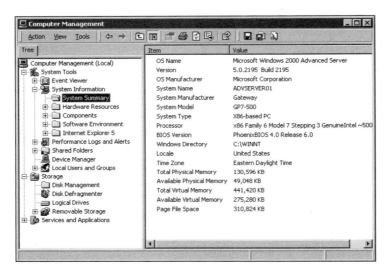

Figure 1-3 Displaying system summary information in Computer Management

5. Using the information from Lab 1.3, determine if the OS, processor and memory on your system meet or exceed the minimum requirements. When checking the memory requirement, compare the amount required to the Available Physical Memory on your system.
6. Expand **Internet Explorer**.
7. Click **Summary** to display the summary information in the right pane.
8. Determine if the version is 5.0 or greater.
9. Close the Computer Management tool by clicking the **Close** button in the top-right corner.
10. On your desktop, right-click **My Computer**, and then click **Explore** from the shortcut menu. The My Computer window appears.
11. Right-click the disk on which SQL Server is to be installed, and then click **Properties** from the shortcut menu. The Local Disk Properties dialog box opens.

Lab 1.4 Determine if your Current Hardware is SQL Server 2000 Compatible 11

12. Click the **General** tab to view the Used and Free space on this disk. Using the information from Lab 1.3, determine if the minimum required amount of hard disk space is available.
13. Click **OK** to close the Local Disk Properties dialog box.
14. Close the My Computer window by clicking the **Close** button in the top-right corner.

Certification Objectives

Objectives for Microsoft Exam #70-228: Installing, Configuring, and Administering Microsoft SQL Server 2000 Enterprise Edition:

➤ Installing and configuring SQL Server 2000

Review Questions

1. What administrative tool is used to view the System Summary information?
   a. Event Viewer
   b. Computer Management
   c. Component Services
   d. Distributed File System

2. System Information can be saved in either a System Info file or a(n):
   a. Excel spreadsheet
   b. Word document
   c. WordPad document
   d. text document

3. System Information can be exported as what type of file?
   a. Text (tab delimited)
   b. Text (comma delimited)
   c. Both a and b

4. What tool is used to determine the available hard disk space?
   a. Windows Explorer
   b. Calculator
   c. Notepad
   d. System Information

5. What tools are available in the Tools tab of the Local Disk Properties dialog box?
   a. Error checking
   b. Backup
   c. Defragmentation
   d. All of the above

CHAPTER TWO

INSTALLING AND UPGRADING SQL SERVER 2000

Labs included in this chapter

- Lab 2.1 Creating a User Account
- Lab 2.2 Installing Microsoft SQL Server 2000
- Lab 2.3 Viewing System Changes Made by SQL Server 2000 Installation
- Lab 2.4 Installing a Second Instance of Microsoft SQL Server 2000
- Lab 2.5 Viewing System Changes Made by Installation of a Second Instance of SQL Server 2000
- Lab 2.6 Uninstalling a Second Instance of SQL Server 2000
- Lab 2.7 Creating an Unattended Installation File
- Lab 2.8 Rebuilding the Registry

Microsoft MCSE Exam #70-228 Objectives	
Objective	Lab
Install SQL Server 2000. Considerations include clustering, default collation, file locations, number of instances, and service accounts	2.1, 2.2, 2.4
Configure network libraries	2.2

LAB 2.1 CREATING A USER ACCOUNT

Objectives

The goal of this lab is to create the user accounts needed for the SQL Server 2000 installation.

Materials Required

This lab will require the following:

➤ Access to a computer running Windows 2000 Server, Windows 2000 Advanced Server, or Windows 2000 Datacenter Server

➤ An operating system user account and password with the right to create user accounts

Estimated completion time: **15 minutes**

Activity Background

After completing your research into SQL Server 2000 in Chapter 1 of this book, you must take the final step to prepare for the installation, which is the creation of the user account. This user account will be used by SQL Server to determine the security context in which SQL Server will run. It must be created before the installation routine is begun, because you will need to supply it during the installation. If this account is not available at the time of the installation, the local system account must be used. The local system account has the administrative rights on the local machine needed by SQL Server, but has no rights to the rest of the network in which the SQL Server resides. In this lab, you will create one account to be used by both of the SQL Server services—the SQL Server itself and the SQL Server Agent—as is done in a typical SQL Server installation. This account should be configured with the Password never expires option, which overrides the password policy set for the network. Also, this account requires several rights and permissions that will be set by the installation routine. You will verify these settings in a later lab. You will then create a second account to be used in a second installation of SQL Server. If you are familiar with the creation of user accounts, and are interested in a challenge, create the accounts on your own without the use of the steps below. Use SQLServerUA and SQLServerUA2 for the names of the accounts, and SQLServerPWD for the passwords.

Activity

1. Boot your computer and log on by pressing **Ctrl+Alt+Del**. In the Log On to Windows window, type your user name and password in the text boxes, and then press **Enter**. The Windows 2000 desktop appears on your screen.

2. Click **Start**, point to **Programs**, point to **Administrative Tools**, and then click **Computer Management**. The Computer Management window appears.

3. Expand **Local Users and Groups**. Click the **Users** folder to display the users created by the installation of the Windows 2000 Server operating system in the right pane.
4. Click the **Action** menu, and then click **New User**. The New User dialog box opens.
5. In the User name text box, type **SQLServerUA**. In the Password and Confirm password text boxes, type **SQLServerPWD**. Remember that passwords are case sensitive. The Full name and Description fields are optional.
6. Click to uncheck the check box to the left of **User must change password at next logon**. This will subsequently allow the User cannot change password and Password never expires options. Click the check box to the left of **Password never expires** (see Figure 2-1).

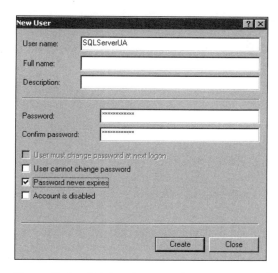

Figure 2-1 Setting Password never expires for a user account in the New User dialog box

7. Click **Create** to complete the creation of this user account.
8. Repeat Steps 5 through 7 to create a second account. Use SQLServerUA2 for the user name. Keep all other settings the same.
9. Click **Close** to close the New User dialog box.
10. To close the Computer Management console, click the **Close** button in the top-right corner of the window.

Certification Objectives

Objectives for Microsoft Exam #70-228: Installing, Configuring, and Administering Microsoft SQL Server 2000 Enterprise Edition:

▶ Install SQL Server 2000. Considerations include clustering, default collation, file locations, number of instances, and service accounts

Review Questions

1. Where can you find the Local Users and Groups tool?
   a. Control Panel
   b. Computer Management
   c. Configure Your Server
   d. Component Services

2. When creating a user account, how do you make the Password never expires option available?
   a. Leave the password blank.
   b. Set the Password never expires option in the password policy for the workgroup or domain.
   c. Uncheck User must change password at next logon.
   d. Check Account is disabled.

3. The user account used by SQL Server and SQL Server Agent must be a member of which group?
   a. Users
   b. Backup Operators
   c. Power Users
   d. Administrators

4. Why is the local system account not used in most SQL Server installations?
   a. It is not a member of the local Administrator group.
   b. It is not a member of the domain Administrator group.
   c. It does not have access to any network resource other than the SQL Server.
   d. It does not have access to the SQL Server computer.

5. What additional rights must you grant to the account used by the SQL Server?
   a. Log on locally
   b. Log on as a service
   c. Access this computer from the network
   d. None of the above

LAB 2.2 INSTALLING MICROSOFT SQL SERVER 2000

Objectives

The goal of this lab is to install SQL Server 2000.

Materials Required

This lab will require the following:

➤ Access to a computer running Windows 2000 Server, Windows 2000 Advanced Server, or Windows 2000 Datacenter Server

➤ Access to the Microsoft SQL Server 2000 installation files

➤ An operating system user account and password with the right to install software applications

➤ The SQLServerUA user account, created in Lab 2.1

Estimated completion time: **45 minutes**

Activity Background

You are now ready to install SQL Server 2000. To do so, you will use the custom installation type. This will allow you to view all the decisions made during a typical installation and become more familiar with the steps performed by the installation routine. You will also be required to supply the user account created in Lab 2.1.

ACTIVITY

1. Boot your computer and log on, if necessary.
2. Click **Start**, and then click **Run**. The Run dialog box opens.
3. Click **Browse**, and navigate to the directory containing the installation files or to the root of the CD. Click the **autorun** program, and then click **Open**. Click **OK** in the Run dialog box. The SQL Server installation routine starts. The initial screen is shown in Figure 2-2.
4. Click **SQL Server 2000 Components**. The installation menu screen appears.
5. Click **Install Database Server**. The Welcome dialog box opens.
6. Click **Next**. The Computer Name dialog box opens.
7. Click **Local Computer**, and then click **Next**. The Installation Selection dialog box opens.

Figure 2-2 SQL Server installation screen

8. Verify that **Create a new instance of SQL Server, or install Client Tools** is selected, and then click **Next**. The User Information dialog box opens.

9. If necessary, enter your name and company name, and then click **Next**. The software License Agreement dialog box opens.

10. Read the agreement, and then click **Yes**. The Installation Definition dialog box opens.

11. Verify that **Server and Client Tools** is selected, and then click **Next**. The Instance Name dialog box opens.

12. Verify that **Default** is checked, and then click **Next**. The Setup Type dialog box opens.

13. In the top third of this screen, click the **Custom** radio button. In the middle third, note the default destination folders. In the bottom third, verify that the required space is available on the program files drive, system drive, and data files drive. Click **Next**. The Select Components dialog box opens.

14. Click each of the Components in the left pane to view the Sub-Components in the right pane. Do not uncheck the boxes, but simply click the text to see the list of sub-components for each component.

15. If you completed Lab 1.2, uncheck the box for **Books Online** (as shown in Figure 2-3). Click **Next**. The Services Accounts dialog box opens.

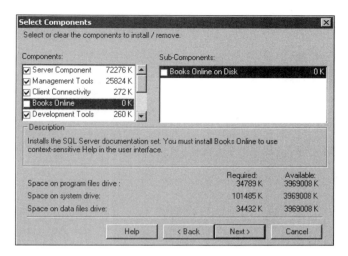

Figure 2-3 Select Components dialog box

16. Verify that the **Use the same account for each service** and the **Use a Domain User account** radio buttons are selected. Delete any text in the Username text box, and type **SQLServerUA**. Type **SQLServerPWD** in the Password text box. Because you are working in a workgroup (not a domain), the name of your computer should be displayed in the Domain text box. If it is not, type the name of your computer in the Domain text box, as shown in Figure 2-4. Click **Next**. The Authentication Mode dialog box opens.

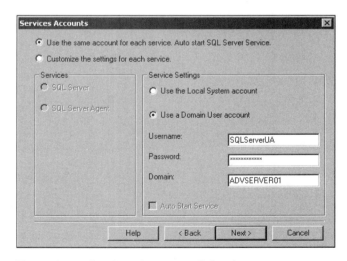

Figure 2-4 Services Accounts dialog box

17. Verify that **Windows Authentication Mode** is selected, and then click **Next**. The Collation Settings dialog box opens.

18. Verify that **SQL Collations** is selected, and **Dictionary order, case-insensitive, for use with 1252 Character Set** is highlighted in the list, and then click **Next**. The Network Libraries dialog box opens.

19. Verify that the check boxes for both Named Pipes and TCP/IP Sockets are checked. Verify that the Named Pipe name is \\.\pipe\sql\query and the Port number is 1433 (as shown in Figure 2-5). Click **Next**. The Start Copying Files dialog box opens.

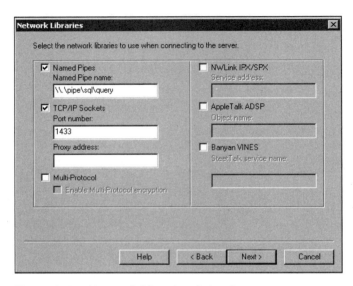

Figure 2-5 Network Libraries dialog box

20. Click **Next**. The installation routine will display several screens as it copies files and performs the installation, ending with the Setup Complete dialog box.

21. Click **Continue** if the SQL Server Licensing Modes screen appears.

 Depending on your computer's configuration, you may or may not see additional screens concerning the installation of the Microsoft Data Access Components (MDAC). If so, click Next to continue the installation.

Certification Objectives

Objectives for Microsoft Exam #70-228: Installing, Configuring, and Administering Microsoft SQL Server 2000 Enterprise Edition:

➤ Install SQL Server 2000. Considerations include clustering, default collation, file locations, number of instances, and service accounts

➤ Configure network libraries

Review Questions

1. Which SQL Server 2000 component is designed to facilitate online analytical processing and data-mining applications?
   a. Analysis Services
   b. English Query
   c. Query Analyzer
   d. Profiler

2. Which option should you choose in the Installation Selection dialog box to install SQL Server 2000?
   a. Install SQL Server
   b. Create a new instance of SQL Server, or install Client Tools
   c. Upgrade, remove, or add components to an existing instance of SQL Server
   d. Advanced Options

3. Which option should you choose in the Installation Definition dialog box to install SQL Server 2000?
   a. Install SQL Server
   b. Client Tools Only
   c. Server and Client Tools
   d. Connectivity Only

4. Which component is the only component not automatically installed during a custom installation?
   a. Server Components
   b. Management Tools
   c. Development Tools
   d. Code Samples

5. What is (are) the default Network Libraries?
   a. Named Pipes
   b. TCP/IP Sockets
   c. Named Pipes and TCP/IP Sockets
   d. NWLink IPX/SPX

Lab 2.3 Viewing System Changes Made by SQL Server 2000 Installation

Objectives

The goal of this lab is to view the changes made to your system due to the installation of SQL Server 2000.

Materials Required

This lab will require the following:

▶ Access to a computer running Windows 2000 Server, Windows 2000 Advanced Server, or Windows 2000 Datacenter Server with Microsoft SQL Server 2000 installed

▶ An operating system user account and password with the right to run Registry Editor (Regedt32)

Estimated completion time: **30 minutes**

Activity Background

Before you begin using SQL Server, take a minute to view the changes made to your computer. In this lab, you will use Windows Explorer to view the directories created, use Regedt32 to view the Registry entries created, view the SQL client tools created, and use Service Manager to view the services created. Finally, you will run Performance Monitor to view the new performance counters added specifically for the SQL Server. Performance Monitor, which is a tool included with the Windows 2000 Server operating system, is used to view the current performance of a system, find possible bottlenecks, and improve the overall performance of a system.

Activity

To use Windows Explorer to view directories created during SQL Server 2000 installation:

1. Boot your computer and log on, if necessary.
2. Click **Start**, point to **Programs**, point to **Accessories**, and then click **Windows Explorer**. The Windows Explorer window appears.
3. Expand **My Computer**.
4. Expand the drive letter where SQL Server was installed (in Lab 2.2), expand the **Program Files** folder, expand the **Microsoft SQL Server** folder, and then expand the **MSSQL** folder. Notice the folders contained in the MSSQL folder (shown in Figure 2-6).

Lab 2.3 Viewing System Changes Made by SQL Server 2000 Installation

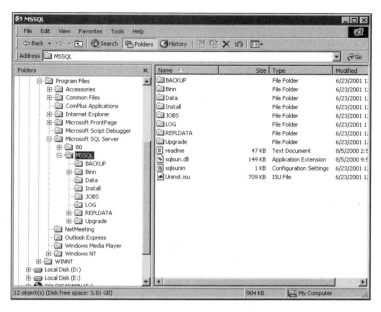

Figure 2-6 Exploring the MSSQL folder

5. Right-click the **MSSQL** folder, and then click **Properties**. The MSSQL Properties dialog box opens. Click the **Security** tab. Notice the SQLServerUA user account has been added to the list of names and has the full control permission for this folder.

6. Click **Cancel** to close the MSSQL Properties dialog box.

7. To close Windows Explorer, click the **Close** button in the top-right corner of the window.

To use Regedt32 to view Registry entries:

1. Click **Start**, and then click **Run**. The Run dialog box opens.

2. Type **regedt32**, and then click **OK**. The Registry Editor window appears.

3. Click the **Options** menu, and then click **Read Only Mode**. This eliminates the chance of inadvertently editing the registry.

4. Click the title bar of the HKEY_LOCAL_MACHINE on Local Machine window to make that window active.

5. Double-click **System**, double-click **CurrentControlSet**, and then double-click **Services**. Scroll to locate and double-click **MSSQLSERVER** (as shown in Figure 2-7).

Chapter 2   Installing and Upgrading SQL Server 2000

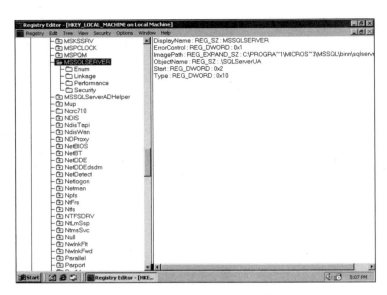

Figure 2-7 Viewing the Registry key MSSQLSERVER

6. Read through the folders and Registry entries listed. You may want to maximize the windows to facilitate easier reading of the Registry keys.

7. Click the **Security** menu, and then click **Permissions**. A security window appears indicating that you have permission only to view the current security information. Click **OK**. The Permissions for MSSQLSERVER dialog box opens. Notice that the SQLServerUA account has been added to this list. Click **Cancel** to close the Permissions for MSSQLSERVER dialog box.

8. Continuing in the Services folder, scroll down further to locate and double-click **SQLSERVERAGENT**.

9. Read through the folders and Registry entries listed.

10. Click the **Security** menu, and then click **Permissions**. A security window appears indicating that you have permission only to view the current security information. Click **OK**. The Permissions for SQLSERVERAGENT dialog box opens. Notice that the SQLServerUA account has not been added to this list. Click **Cancel** to close the Permissions for SQLSERVERAGENT dialog box.

11. To close Registry Editor, click the **Close** button in the top-right corner of the window.

To view the SQL Server Service Manager:

1. Click **Start**, point to **Programs**, and then point to **Microsoft SQL Server**. Listed in this submenu are all the tools installed along with the SQL Server database engine. Click **Service Manager**. The SQL Server Service Manager window appears, as shown in Figure 2-8.

Lab 2.3 Viewing System Changes Made by SQL Server 2000 Installation

Figure 2-8 SQL Server Service Manager window

2. Ensure that the SQL Server Service Manager is running – if it is stopped, this will be indicated by a red square. If a red square is present, click the **Services** list arrow and then select **SQL Server** and **SQL Server Agent**.

3. To close SQL Server Service Manager, click the **Close** button in the top-right corner of the window.

To use Performance Monitor:

1. Click **Start**, point to **Programs**, point to **Administrative Tools**, and then click **Performance**. The Performance window appears.

2. Verify that System Monitor is selected in the Tree pane, and then click the **Add** button (+) in the Details pane. The Add Counters dialog box opens.

3. Click the **Performance object** list arrow, and view the counters listed for the SQL Server. Click each of the Performance objects for the SQL Server, and view the counters available for each object. For example, choose the **SQL Server:Databases** object, and notice the **Percent Log Used** counter, as shown in Figure 2-9. This counter is especially handy to ensure that a log file does not become full.

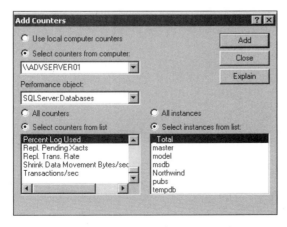

Figure 2-9 Viewing the SQL Server databases counters in Performance Monitor

4. Click **Close** to close the Add Counters dialog box.

5. To close Performance Monitor, click the **Close** button in the top-right corner of the window.

Review Questions

1. Where do you find the folder used to store the majority of the files needed for the SQL Server?
   a. On the root of the drive used to install SQL Server
   b. In the Documents and Settings folder
   c. In the Program Files folder
   d. In the folder used to store the Windows 2000 operating systems files (usually named WINNT)

2. What is the value of the ObjectName key in the Registry path HKEY_LOCAL_MACHINE/System/CurrentControlSet/Services/MSSQLServer?
   a. MSSQL\binn\sqlservr.exe
   b. SQLServerUA
   c. MSSQL\binn\sqlagent.exe
   d. 0x3

3. For which registry sub-key does the SQLServerUA account have the Full Control permission?
   a. MSSQLSERVER
   b. SQLBINAGENT
   c. MSSQLSTATION
   d. None of the above

4. Which tool could you use to set the SQLSERVERAGENT service to autostart when the operating system starts?
   a. Books Online
   b. Client Network Utility
   c. Profiler
   d. Service Manager

5. Which Performance Monitor counter tracks the number of users connected to the system?
   a. SQLServer:Databases:Active Transactions
   b. SQLServer:Databases:Transactions/sec
   c. SQLServer:General Statistics:User Connections
   d. SQLServer:General Statistics:Logins/sec

Lab 2.4 Installing a Second Instance of Microsoft SQL Server 2000

Objectives

The goal of this lab is to install a second instance of SQL Server 2000.

Materials Required

This lab will require the following:

- Access to a computer running Windows 2000 Server, Windows 2000 Advanced Server, or Windows 2000 Datacenter Server with Microsoft SQL Server 2000 installed (completed in Lab 2.2)
- Access to the Microsoft SQL Server 2000 installation files
- An operating system user account and password with the right to install software applications
- The SQLServerUA2 user account, created in Lab 2.1

Estimated completion time: **30 minutes**

Activity Background

It is often advantageous to have multiple instances of SQL Server on a single computer, perhaps when both a test and live version of the same environment are needed, or when different versions of SQL Server (6.5, 7.0, and 2000) are required. In this lab, you will install a second instance of SQL Server 2000, with a typical configuration.

Activity

1. Boot your computer and log on, if necessary.
2. Click **Start**, and then click **Run**. The Run dialog box opens.
3. Click **Browse**, and navigate to the directory containing the installation files or the root of the CD. Click the **autorun** program, and then click **Open**. Click **OK** in the Run dialog box. The SQL Server installation routine starts.
4. Click **SQL Server 2000 Components**. The installation menu screen appears.
5. Click **Install Database Server**. The Welcome dialog box opens.
6. Click **Next**. The Computer Name dialog box opens.
7. Click **Local Computer**, and then click **Next**. The Installation Selection dialog box opens.

8. Verify that **Create a new instance of SQL Server, or install Client Tools** is selected, and then click **Next**. The User Information dialog box opens.

9. If necessary, enter your name and company name, and then click **Next**. The software License Agreement dialog box opens.

10. Read the agreement, and then click **Yes**. The Installation Definition dialog box opens.

11. Verify that **Server and Client Tools** is selected, and then click **Next**. The Instance Name dialog box opens.

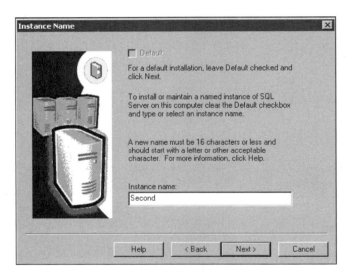

Figure 2-10   Instance Name dialog box

12. In the Instance name text box, type **Second** (as shown in Figure 2-10), and then click **Next**. The Setup Type dialog box opens.

13. Verify that the **Typical** radio button is selected, and then click **Next**. The Services Accounts dialog box opens.

14. Verify that the **Use the same account for each service** and the **Use a Domain User account** radio buttons are selected. Delete any text in the Username text box, and type **SQLServerUA2**. Type **SQLServerPWD** in the Password text box. Because you are working in a workgroup (not a domain), the name of your computer should be displayed in the Domain text box. If it is not, type the name of your computer in the Domain text box. Click **Next**. The Authentication Mode dialog box opens.

15. Verify that **Windows Authentication Mode** is selected, and then click **Next**. The Start Copying Files dialog box opens.

16. Click **Next**. The Microsoft Data Access Components 2.6 Setup dialog box opens. You may need to click **Continue** if the SQL Server Licensing Modes screen appears.

17. Click **Next**, and then click **Finish** to shut down the first instance of SQL Server and continue with the installation. The installation routine will display several screens as it copies files and performs the installation, ending with the Setup Complete dialog box.

Certification Objectives

Objectives for Microsoft Exam #70-228: Installing, Configuring, and Administering Microsoft SQL Server 2000 Enterprise Edition:

➤ Install SQL Server 2000. Considerations include clustering, default collation, file locations, number of instances, and service accounts

Review Questions

1. What is the maximum number of characters for an instance name?
   a. 10
   b. 12
   c. 16
   d. 20

2. In the Instance name dialog box, if the default instance check box is cleared, Setup has detected a default instance of SQL Server on the computer. The default instance could be:
   a. SQL Server 6.5
   b. SQL Server 7.0
   c. The default instance of SQL Server 2000
   d. All of the above

3. Which configuration setting can be set in a custom installation and is not available in a typical installation?
   a. Services Accounts
   b. Network Libraries
   c. Authentication Mode
   d. Destination Folders

4. In which type of Setup can you choose a Collation setting (other than the default)?
   a. Typical
   b. Minimum
   c. Custom
   d. Compact

5. When you use the same account for each service, which service is automatically started?
   a. SQL Server
   b. SQL Server Agent
   c. MS Search
   d. All of the above

LAB 2.5 VIEWING SYSTEM CHANGES MADE BY INSTALLATION OF A SECOND INSTANCE OF SQL SERVER 2000

Objectives

The goal of this lab is to view the changes made to your system due to the installation of a second instance of SQL Server 2000.

Materials Required

This lab will require the following:

➤ Access to a computer running Microsoft Windows 2000 Server, Windows 2000 Advanced Server, or Windows 2000 Datacenter Server with Microsoft SQL Server 2000 installed twice (completed in Labs 2.2 and 2.4)

➤ An operating system user account and password with the right to run Registry Editor (Regedt32)

Estimated completion time: 20 minutes

Activity Background

The ability to have multiple named instances of SQL Server 2000 is a powerful feature. Being aware of the shared and separate resources generated by having multiple instances is a must for any SQL Server administrator. In this lab, you will view both the shared resources between the instances (the Management tool, for example), and the separate resources (the Registry keys, for example) that are generated by the installation of a second instance of SQL Server 2000.

ACTIVITY

To view the new folder MSSQL$SECOND:

1. Boot your computer and log on, if necessary.
2. Click **Start**, point to **Programs**, point to **Accessories**, and then click **Windows Explorer**. The Windows Explorer window appears.
3. Expand **My Computer**.

Lab 2.5 Viewing System Changes Made by Installation of a Second Instance of SQL

4. Expand the drive letter where SQL Server was installed (in Lab 2.2). Expand the **Program Files** folder, and then expand the **Microsoft SQL Server** folder. Notice the new folder MSSQL$SECOND.

5. To close Windows Explorer, click the **Close** button in the top-right corner of the window.

To view Registry entry changes using Regedt32:

1. Click **Start**, and then click **Run**. The Run dialog box opens.

2. Type **regedt32**, and then click **OK**. The Registry Editor window appears.

3. If you have not completed Lab 2.3, click the **Options** menu, and then click **Read Only Mode**. This eliminates the chance of inadvertently editing the Registry.

4. Click the title bar of the HKEY_LOCAL_MACHINE on the Local Machine window to make that window active.

5. Double-click **System**, double-click **CurrentControlSet**, and then double-click **Services**. Scroll down to locate MSSQL$SECOND and MSSQLSERVER. Double-click **MSSQL$SECOND**, and read through the folders and Registry entries listed (as shown in Figure 2-11). You may want to maximize the windows to facilitate easier reading of the Registry keys.

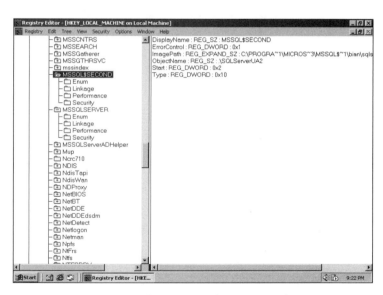

Figure 2-11 Viewing the Registry key MSSQL$SECOND

6. Continuing in the Services folder, scroll down further to locate SQLAgent$Second and SQLSERVERAGENT.

7. Double-click **SQLAgent$Second**, and read through the folders and Registry entries listed.

8. To close Registry Editor, click the **Close** button in the top-right corner of the window.

To view SQL Server services:

1. Click **Start**, point to **Programs**, and then point to **Microsoft SQL Server**. Notice that only one set of tools is listed. Click **Service Manager**. The SQL Server Service Manager window appears.

2. Notice that the SQL Server Service Manager does not allow the management of the two sets of services.

3. To close SQL Server Service Manager, click the **Close** button in the top-right corner of the window.

4. Click **Start**, point to **Programs**, point to **Administrative Tools**, and then click **Services**. The Services window appears.

5. Scroll through the list of services to view the two SQL Server and SQL Server Agent services.

6. To close the Services window, click the **Close** button in the top-right corner of the window.

Review Questions

1. What is the name of the folder used to store the majority of the files needed for the second SQL Server instance (named Second)?
   a. MSSQL
   b. SECOND$MSSQL
   c. MSSQL$SECOND
   d. MS SQL Server Second Instance

2. What is the name of the Registry key used to store the majority of the entries needed for the second SQL Server instance (named Second)?
   a. MS SQL Server Second Instance
   b. MSSQL
   c. SECOND$MSSQL
   d. MSSQL$SECOND

3. What tool is used to view and manage the services when multiple instances of SQL Server are installed?
   a. Service Manager
   b. Services
   c. Books Online
   d. Profiler

4. What is the name of the service for the SQL Server Agent of the second SQL Server instance (named Second)?
   a. SQLAgent$SECOND
   b. SQLSERVERAGENT$SECOND
   c. SECOND$SQLAgent
   d. MSSQLSQLAgent$SECOND

5. If you have SQL Server 7.0 installed, and you install SQL Server 2000 as a second named instance, what version of Books Online and the other client tools will you have?
   a. 6.5
   b. 7.0
   c. 2000
   d. Both 7.0 and 2000

LAB 2.6 UNINSTALLING A SECOND INSTANCE OF SQL SERVER 2000

Objectives

The goal of this lab is to uninstall the second instance of SQL Server 2000.

Materials Required

This lab will require the following:

➤ Access to a computer running Windows 2000 Server, Windows 2000 Advanced Server, or Windows 2000 Datacenter Server with Microsoft SQL Server 2000 installed twice (completed in Labs 2.2 and 2.4)

➤ An operating system user account and password with the right to install and uninstall software applications

Estimated completion time: 15 minutes

Activity Background

Now that you have gained some experience with using multiple named instances of SQL Server 2000, you no longer need the second instance. In this lab, you will use the Add/Remove Programs applet in Control Panel to uninstall the second instance of SQL Server.

ACTIVITY

1. Boot your computer and log on, if necessary.

2. Click **Start**, point to **Settings**, and then click **Control Panel**. The Control Panel window appears.

3. Double-click **Add/Remove Programs**. The Add/Remove Programs window appears, as shown in Figure 2-12.

Figure 2-12   Add/Remove Programs window

4. Verify that the **Change or Remove Programs** option is selected (on the left side of the screen). Click **Microsoft SQL Server 2000 (SECOND)**, and then click **Change/Remove**. The Confirm File Deletion dialog box opens.

5. Click **Yes**. The Remove Programs From Your Computer dialog box opens. If the Remove Shared File? dialog box opens asking if you wish to remove a file, Click **No**. You should choose this option because it is the safest choice, especially if other software packages are installed on this machine.

6. Click **OK** in the Remove Programs From Your Computer dialog box, and then click **Close** in the Add/Remove Programs window.

7. Click **Start**, and then click **Shut Down**. The Shut Down Windows dialog box opens. Click the drop-down list arrow, click **Restart** if necessary, and then click **OK** to restart your computer.

 The Add/Remove Programs applet does not require this reboot, but it is always a good idea to ensure that any file deletions and Registry changes are fully completed before continuing to use your system.

Review Questions

1. What tool is used to uninstall the second instance of SQL Server?
    a. Add/Remove Hardware
    b. Add/Remove Programs

c. Computer Management
   d. Configure Your Server
2. Which option in the Add/Remove Programs window is used to uninstall the second instance of SQL Server?
   a. Change or Remove Programs
   b. Add New Programs
   c. Add/Remove Windows Components
   d. Uninstall Software
3. What is the safest thing to do in response to the question posed in the Remove Shared File? dialog box?
   a. Click Yes
   b. Click Yes to All
   c. Click No
   d. Click OK
4. Why should you reboot your system after uninstalling the second instance of SQL Server 2000?
   a. It is required by the Add/Remove Programs applet.
   b. The default SQL Server 2000 will be unusable until you do so.
   c. The SQL Server Client Tools will be unavailable until you to so.
   d. This ensures file deletions and Registry changes are fully completed.
5. What information is not listed in the Support Info dialog box (obtained by clicking the support information link in the Add/Remove Programs dialog box)?
   a. Size
   b. Version
   c. Registered Company
   d. Registered Owner

LAB 2.7 CREATING AN UNATTENDED INSTALLATION FILE

Objectives

The goal of this lab is to create an unattended installation file.

Materials Required

This lab will require the following:

- Access to a computer running Microsoft Windows 2000 Server, Windows 2000 Advanced Server, or Windows 2000 Datacenter Server with Microsoft SQL Server 2000 installed (completed in Lab 2.2)
- An operating system user account and password with the right to install software applications

36 Chapter 2 Installing and Upgrading SQL Server 2000

Estimated completion time: 20 minutes

Activity Background

The ability to perform an unattended installation of SQL Server 2000 is a handy feature, especially if you are responsible for servers in remote locations or for several servers that are to have the exact same configuration. You can also use the unattended installation feature to install the client tools on several machines. The first step in an unattended installation on is the creation of the unattended installation file. There are several ways to create this file, and in this lab you will use the setup program to create one for you. If you are interested in a challenge, create the file without the use of the steps below. Remember, creation of an unattended installation file is an Advanced Option.

You can use Books Online to research the various batch files used to perform unattended installations.

ACTIVITY

1. Boot your computer and log on, if necessary.
2. Click **Start**, and then click **Run**. The Run dialog box opens.
3. Click **Browse**, and navigate to the directory containing the installation files or to the root of the CD. Click the **autorun** program, and then click **Open**. Click **OK** in the Run dialog box. The SQL Server installation routine starts.
4. Click **SQL Server 2000 Components**. The installation menu screen appears.
5. Click **Install Database Server**. The Welcome dialog box opens.
6. Click **Next**. The Computer Name dialog box opens.
7. Click **Local Computer** if necessary, and then click **Next**. The Installation Selection dialog box opens.
8. Click **Advanced options**, and then click **Next**. The Advanced Options dialog box opens.
9. Click **Record Unattended .ISS file** (as shown in Figure 2-13), and then click **Next**. The User Information dialog box opens.

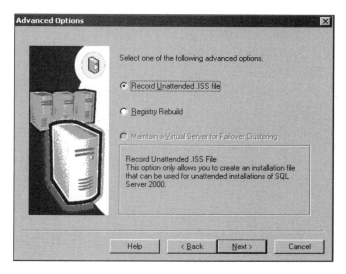

Figure 2-13 Advanced Options dialog box with Record Unattended .ISS file option selected

10. If necessary, enter your name and company name, and then click **Next**. The software License Agreement dialog box opens.

11. Read the agreement, and then click **Yes**. The Installation Definition dialog box opens.

12. Click **Client Tools Only**, and then click **Next**. The Select Components dialog box opens.

13. Click **Next**. The Start Copying Files dialog box opens.

14. Click **Next**. The Setup Complete dialog box opens.

Review Questions

1. What tool is used to create the unattended installation file?
   a. Client Network Utility
   b. Enterprise Manager
   c. Server Network Utility
   d. The Setup program included with the SQL Server installation files

2. What is the three-letter extension of the unattended installation file?
   a. .iss
   b. .sis
   c. .ssi
   d. .uif

3. Where is the unattended installation file saved?
   a. On the root of the drive used to install SQL Server
   b. In the Documents and Settings folder
   c. In the Program Files folder
   d. In the folder used to store the Windows 2000 operating systems files (usually named WINNT)
4. After your unattended installation file has been created, which batch file (supplied with the SQL Server installation files) would you use to perform a standard installation?
   a. Squif.bat
   b. Sqlins.bat
   c. Sqlcli.bat
   d. Sqlcst.bat
5. After your unattended installation file has been created, which batch file (supplied with the SQL Server installation files) would you use to perform a client-only installation?
   a. Squif.bat
   b. Sqlins.bat
   c. Sqlcli.bat
   d. Sqlcst.bat

LAB 2.8 REBUILDING THE REGISTRY

Objectives

The goal of this lab is to rebuild the Registry of a damaged system using the SQL Server Setup program.

Materials Required

This lab will require the following:

➤ Access to a computer running Windows 2000 Server, Windows 2000 Advanced Server, or Windows 2000 Datacenter Server with Microsoft SQL Server 2000 installed (completed in Lab 2.2)

➤ An operating system user account and password with the right to install software applications

➤ Access to the Microsoft SQL Server 2000 installation files

Lab 2.8 Rebuilding the Registry 39

Estimated completion time: **25 minutes**

Activity Background

In a perfect world, your SQL Server would run smoothly, and never fail. Unfortunately, life isn't so easy, and as a SQL Server administrator, you need to be prepared for the worst. The Registry is the configuration database for both SQL and Windows 2000, as well as any other application installed on your system. In this lab, you will use the setup program that accompanies the SQL Server installation files to repair an ailing system. As a challenge, repair the system without the use of the steps below. Remember, the Registry rebuild utility is an Advanced Option.

ACTIVITY

1. Boot your computer and log on, if necessary.
2. Click **Start**, and then click **Run**. The Run dialog box opens.
3. Click **Browse**, and navigate to the directory containing the installation files or to the root of the CD. Click the **autorun** program, and then click **Open**. Click **OK** in the Run dialog box. The SQL Server installation routine starts
4. Click **SQL Server 2000 Components**. The installation menu screen appears.
5. Click **Install Database Server**. The Welcome dialog box opens.
6. Click **Next**. The Computer Name dialog box opens.
7. Click **Local Computer** if necessary, and then click **Next**. The Installation Selection dialog box opens.
8. Click **Advanced options**, and then click **Next**. The Advanced Options dialog box opens.
9. Click **Registry Rebuild** (as shown in Figure 2-14), and then click **Next**. The Setup dialog box opens with a message stating that Setup will rebuild your Registry based on information that you supply.

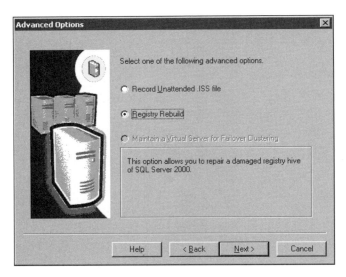

Figure 2-14 Advanced Options dialog box with Registry Rebuild option selected

10. Click **OK**. The User Information dialog box opens.

11. If necessary, enter your name and company name, and then click **Next**. The software License Agreement dialog box opens.

12. Read the agreement, and then click **Yes**. The Installation Definition dialog box opens.

13. Verify that **Server and Client Tools** is selected, and then click **Next**. The Instance Name dialog box opens.

14. Verify that **Default** is checked, and then click **Next**. The Setup Type dialog box opens.

15. Click **Custom**, and then click **Next**. The Select Components dialog box opens.

16. If you unchecked Books Online in the original installation (in Lab 2.2), uncheck it here, and then click **Next**.

17. Verify that the **Use the same account for each service** and the **Use a Domain User account** radio buttons are selected. Delete any text in the Username text box, and type **SQLServerUA**. Type **SQLServerPWD** in the Password text box. Because you are working in a workgroup (not a domain), the name of your computer should be displayed in the Domain text box. If it is not, type the name of your computer in the Domain text box. Click **Next**. The Authentication Mode dialog box opens.

18. Verify that **Windows Authentication Mode** is selected, and then click **Next**. The Collation Settings dialog box opens.

19. Verify that **SQL Collations** is selected, and **Dictionary order, case-insensitive, for use with 1252 Character Set** is highlighted in the list, and then click **Next**. The Network Libraries dialog box opens.
20. Verify that the check boxes for both Named Pipes and TCP/IP Sockets are checked. Do not change the contents of the Named Pipe name and Port number text boxes. Click **Next**. The Setup Information dialog box opens.
21. Click **Next**. The setup routine will display several screens as it repairs the Registry, ending with the Setup Complete dialog box.
22. Click **Finish**. You may need to click **Continue** if the SQL Server Licensing Modes screen appears.

Review Questions

1. What tool is used to rebuild the Registry?
    a. Client Network Utility
    b. Enterprise Manager
    c. Server Network Utility
    d. The Setup program included with the SQL Server installation files

2. Which installation option is used to rebuild the Registry?
    a. Create a new instance of SQL Server, or install Client Tools
    b. Upgrade, remove, or add components to an existing instance of SQL Server
    c. Advanced Options
    d. Repair Options

3. The Registry repair option rebuilds the Registry based on information you supply. If you do not have the exact settings used in the original install, what should you do?
    a. Uninstall and reinstall.
    b. Repair the Registry using Enterprise Manager.
    c. Repair the Registry using Add/Remove Programs.
    d. Guess.

4. Rebuilding the Registry includes recopying which external components?
    a. MDAC
    b. MS DTC
    c. MS Search
    d. MDAC and MS DTC

5. What is the name of the 32-bit registry editor program?
    a. Regedit
    b. Regedt32
    c. Regedit32
    d. Regedt

CHAPTER THREE

Administering and Configuring SQL Server 2000

Labs included in this chapter

- Lab 3.1 Viewing the Properties of SQL Server Using Enterprise Manager
- Lab 3.2 Using the SQL Query Analyzer
- Lab 3.3 Using the Sp_configure System Stored Procedure to Alter Configuration Settings
- Lab 3.4 Creating a Linked Server Using Enterprise Manager
- Lab 3.5 Using the Osql Utility
- Lab 3.6 Using the Sqldiag Utility

Microsoft MCSE Exam #70-228 Objectives

Objective	Lab
Create a Linked Server	3.4

LAB 3.1 VIEWING THE PROPERTIES OF SQL SERVER USING ENTERPRISE MANAGER

Objectives

The goal of this lab is to become familiar with Enterprise Manager, and to use it to view the properties of your SQL Server.

Materials Required

This lab will require the following:

> ➤ Access to a computer running Windows 2000 Server, Windows 2000 Advanced Server, or Windows 2000 Datacenter Server with SQL Server 2000 installed

Estimated completion time: **20 minutes**

Activity Background

Now that SQL Server has been installed, you must begin configuring it. The most important and most used tool of those installed with your server is Enterprise Manager. A thorough understanding of Enterprise Manager and its capabilities is required knowledge for any SQL Server administrator. In this lab, you will become familiar with many of the configuration options simply by reading the multiple tabs of the Properties page for your server. If at any time you need some extra help on any of the configuration options listed in a dialog box, press F1 to evoke SQL Server Books Online.

ACTIVITY

1. Boot your computer and log on, if necessary.

2. Click **Start**, point to **Programs**, point to **Microsoft SQL Server**, and then click **Enterprise Manager**. The SQL Server Enterprise Manager window appears.

3. Expand **Microsoft SQL Servers**, expand **SQL Server Group**, and then expand your *server_name*.

4. Right-click to highlight your server, and then click **Properties**. The SQL Server Properties (Configure) dialog box opens. Click the **General** tab, as shown in Figure 3-1.

5. Read through the information listed on this screen, specifically noting the Autostart policies. Click **Startup Parameters**. The Startup Parameters dialog box opens.

6. Press **F1** to evoke Books Online. Click **Using Startup Options**. Read the Books Online document titled "Using Startup Options."

Lab 3.1 Viewing the Properties of SQL Server Using Enterprise Manager

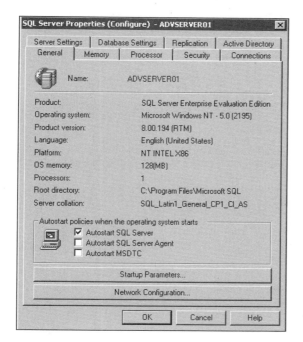

Figure 3-1 The SQL Server Properties (Configure) dialog box

7. To close Books Online, click the **Close** button in the top-right corner of the window.

8. Click **Cancel** to close the Startup Parameters dialog box.

9. Returning to the SQL Server Properties (Configure) dialog box, click **Network Configuration**. The SQL Server Network Utility dialog box opens.

10. Under Enabled protocols, click **Named Pipes**, and then click **Properties**. The Named Pipes dialog box opens.

11. Note the default pipe, and then click **Cancel**.

12. Under Enabled protocols, click **TCP/IP**, and then click **Properties**. The TCP/IP dialog box opens.

13. Note the default port, and then click **Cancel**.

14. Click **Cancel** to close the SQL Server Network Utility dialog box.

15. Returning to the SQL Server Properties (Configure) dialog box, click each tab, one by one. Read through the configuration options displayed on each page. After you have examined all nine tabs, click **Cancel** to close the SQL Server Properties (Configure) dialog box.

16. To close Enterprise Manager, click the **Close** button in the top-right corner of the window.

Review Questions

1. Which tab of the SQL Server Properties (Configure) dialog box allows you to change the authentication mode for your server?
   a. General
   b. Authentication
   c. Security
   d. Server Settings

2. Which tab of the SQL Server Properties (Configure) dialog box allows you to change the Recovery Interval for your server?
   a. Recovery
   b. Database Settings
   c. Server Settings
   d. General

3. Which tab of the SQL Server Properties (Configure) dialog box allows you to change the Autostart policy for your server?
   a. General
   b. Memory
   c. Processor
   d. Security

4. Which tab of the SQL Server Properties (Configure) dialog box allows you to change the two-digit year support for your server?
   a. General
   b. Processor
   c. Connections
   d. Server Settings

5. Which tab of the SQL Server Properties (Configure) dialog box allows you to change the default database location for your server?
   a. Memory
   b. Database Settings
   c. Processor
   d. Security

LAB 3.2 USING THE SQL QUERY ANALYZER

Objectives

The goal of this lab is to become familiar with T-SQL queries and the Query Analyzer, and execute a simple query against the pubs database.

Materials Required

This lab will require the following:

➤ Access to a computer running Windows 2000 Server, Windows 2000 Advanced Server, or Windows 2000 Datacenter Server with SQL Server 2000 installed

Estimated completion time: 30 minutes

Activity Background

Before you can effectively use Query Analyzer, you must understand what a query is and what it can do for you. In this lab, you will use Books Online to become more familiar with queries, as well as the templates that SQL Server 2000 supplies. These templates will save you much time and aggravation, especially for those of you who do not have much experience with T-SQL, the programming language in which queries are written. You will then create a simple select query, and execute it against the pubs database. Finally, you will view a template to create a basic table.

Activity

1. Boot your computer and log on, if necessary.

2. Click **Start**, point to **Programs**, point to **Microsoft SQL Server**, and then click **Enterprise Manager**. The SQL Server Enterprise Manager window appears.

3. Click the **Tools** menu, and then click **SQL Query Analyzer**. The Connect to SQL Server dialog box opens.

4. Verify that **(local)** is listed in the text box and that the **Windows authentication** radio button is selected, and then click **OK**. The SQL Query Analyzer window appears.

5. Press **F1** to evoke Books Online. Read through the displayed information titled "Overview of SQL Query Analyzer."

6. In the Navigation pane, click the **Search** tab. Type **"Query Fundamentals"** (including the quotes) in the search criteria text box, and then click **List Topics**. The results of the search are displayed.

7. Under Select topic, double-click **Query Fundamentals**. Read through the displayed information titled "Query Fundamentals."

8. To close Books Online, click the **Close** button in the top-right corner of the window. You are returned to the SQL Query Analyzer window.

9. If the Object Browser window is not visible, activate it by pressing **F8**.

10. Under your *servername*, expand the **pubs** database, and then expand the **UserTables** folder.

The pubs and the Northwind databases were created during the installation of SQL Server 2000. These two databases are for demonstration, learning, and testing purposes only. They can be altered, added to, or deleted at any time with no ill effect on your server.

11. Right-click the **dbo.authors** table, and then click **Open**. The Open Table window appears, as shown in Figure 3-2. Scroll through the information stored in this table to become familiar with the rows and columns.

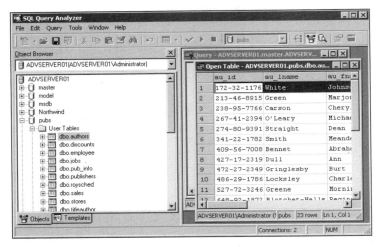

Figure 3-2 The authors table of the pubs database, as seen using Query Analyzer

12. To close the Open Table window, click the **Close** button in the top-right corner of the window. You are returned to the SQL Query Analyzer window.

13. In the toolbar, click the **Database list** arrow, and then click **pubs**. In the query window, type **Select * from authors**, and then press **Enter**.

14. Notice that nothing happens when you press the Enter key. That is because queries can be many lines long, and Query Analyzer is waiting for you to instruct it to execute the query. Press **F5**. The results of your query are displayed in the Results pane.

15. Scroll through the results and notice that they are the same results as those displayed when you opened the table. (The * in your select statement indicates that all columns are to be returned, and the fact that there is no WHERE clause indicates that all rows are to be returned.)

16. At the bottom of the Object Browser window, click the **Templates** tab. The Templates folder is displayed.

17. Expand the **Create Table** folder. Double-click **Create Table Basic Template**. A second query window appears.

18. Read through the T-SQL code. In Chapter 4 of this manual, you will learn more about tables and how to use this code to create a simple table.

19. To close Query Analyzer, click the **Close** button in the top-right corner of the window. The SQL Query Analyzer dialog box opens, asking if you want to save changes.

20. Click **No To All**. You are returned to Enterprise Manager.

21. To close Enterprise Manager, click the **Close** button in the top-right corner of the window.

Review Questions

1. How can you launch Query Analyzer?
    a. From the Start menu
    b. From inside Enterprise Manager
    c. By executing the isql utility
    d. All of the above

2. In a select statement, what is listed in the SELECT list?
    a. Column names
    b. Table names
    c. Database names
    d. Columns that qualify under a certain condition

3. In a select statement, what is listed in the FROM clause?
    a. Column names
    b. Table names
    c. Database names
    d. Columns that qualify under a certain condition

4. In a select statement, what is listed in the WHERE clause?
    a. Column names
    b. Table names
    c. Database names
    d. Columns that qualify under a certain condition

5. What database was created during the SQL Server installation for testing and demonstration purposes only, and can be deleted at any time?
    a. Master
    b. Model
    c. Northwind
    d. Tempdb

Lab 3.3 Using the Sp_configure System Stored Procedure to Alter Configuration Settings

Objectives

The goal of this lab is to become familiar with the system stored procedure sp_configure, and how it can be used to change configuration settings.

Materials Required

This lab will require the following:

> Access to a computer running Windows 2000 Server, Windows 2000 Advanced Server, or Windows 2000 Datacenter Server with SQL Server 2000 installed

Estimated completion time: **30 minutes**

Activity Background

As a SQL Server administrator, you may need to alter the configuration settings for a server. Many of these settings are available through Enterprise Manager. Some, however, are not, and you will need to use the system stored procedure sp_configure to gain access to them. In this lab, you will use Books Online to become more familiar with this statement and the configuration options. You will then use both the system stored procedure and Enterprise Manager to change an option and then reset the option to its original value.

Activity

1. Boot your computer and log on, if necessary.

2. Click **Start**, point to **Programs**, point to **Microsoft SQL Server**, and then click **Query Analyzer**. The Connect to SQL Server window appears.

3. Verify that **(local)** is listed in the SQL Server text box, and that the **Windows authentication** radio button is selected, and then click **OK**. The SQL Query Analyzer window appears.

4. Press **F1** to evoke Books Online.

5. In the Navigation pane, click the **Search** tab. Type **sp_configure** in the search criteria text box, and then click **List Topics**. The results of the search are displayed.

6. Under Select topic, double-click **sp_configure**. Read through the information displayed.

7. Under Select topic, double-click **Setting Configuration Options**. Read through the information displayed.

Lab 3.3 Using the Sp_configure System Stored Procedure to Alter Configuration Settings 51

8. To close Books Online, click the **Close** button in the top-right corner of the window. You are returned to the SQL Query Analyzer window.

9. If the Object Browser window is not visible, activate it by pressing **F8**.

10. In the query window, type the following text:

    exec sp_configure
    go

    and then press **F5**. Some of the configuration options are displayed listing the minimum, maximum, configured, and running values. Notice that recovery interval is not listed.

11. In the query window, edit the previous text to read:

    exec sp_configure 'show advanced options','1'
    go
    reconfigure

    and then press **F5**. The message "DBCC execution completed. If DBCC printed error messages, contact your system administrator. Configuration option 'show advanced options' changed from 0 to 1." is displayed in the Messages tab.

12. In the query window, edit the previous text to read:

    exec sp_configure
    go

    and then press **F5**. Now, all of the configuration options are displayed listing the minimum, maximum, configured, and running values (including recovery interval).

13. Review these settings, taking special note of the value for recovery interval.

14. In the query window, add the following text (under the first two lines):

    exec sp_configure 'recovery interval', '5'
    go

    Highlight these two lines of text, and then press **F5**. The message "DBCC execution completed. If DBCC printed error messages, contact your system administrator. Configuration option 'recovery interval (min)' changed form 0 to 5. Run the RECONFIGURE statement to install." is displayed in the Messages tab.

15. In the query window, add the following text (under the first four lines):

    reconfigure

    Highlight this line of text, and then press **F5**. The message "The command(s) completed successfully." is displayed in the Messages tab.

16. In the query window, highlight the first two lines of text, and then press **F5** to redisplay the configuration values. Scroll down to view the changed value for recovery interval, as shown in Figure 3-3.

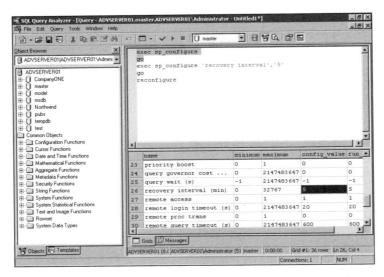

Figure 3-3   Changing the recovery interval using sp_configure

17. Click **Start**, point to **Programs**, point to **Microsoft SQL Server**, and then click **Enterprise Manager**. The SQL Server Enterprise Manager window appears.

18. Expand **Microsoft SQL Servers**. Expand **SQL Server Group**. Expand your *server_name*.

19. Right-click your server, and then click **Properties**. The SQL Server Properties (Configure) dialog box opens. Click the **Database Settings** tab.

20. Type **0** in the Recovery interval (min) text box, and then click **OK**.

21. Return to the SQL Query Analyzer by clicking the **SQL Query Analyzer** button on your taskbar.

22. In the query window, highlight the first two lines of text, and then press **F5** to redisplay the configuration values. Scroll down to view the reset value for recovery interval.

23. To close SQL Query Analyzer, click the **Close** button in the top-right corner of the window. The SQL Query Analyzer dialog box opens, asking if you want to save changes.

24. Click **No To All**. You are returned to Enterprise Manager.

25. To close Enterprise Manager, click the **Close** button in the top-right corner of the window.

Review Questions

1. What are the two arguments for the sp_configure statement?
   a. name and value
   b. configname and configvalue
   c. @name and @value
   d. @configname and @configvalue

2. The sp_configure statement is used to display or change server-level settings. What statement should be used to change database-level settings?
   a. sp_dbconfigure
   b. sp_dboption
   c. sp_database_configure
   d. sp_database_option

3. How can you instruct Query Analyzer to execute a query?
   a. Click Execute under the Query menu
   b. Click the Execute Query button in the toolbar
   c. Press F5
   d. All of the above

4. Which of the following configuration options require a server restart?
   a. Allow updates
   b. Default language
   c. Priority boost
   d. Recovery Interval

5. Which of the following configuration options is a self-configuring option?
   a. Locks
   b. Min memory per query
   c. Using nested triggers
   d. Remote login timeout

LAB 3.4 CREATING A LINKED SERVER USING ENTERPRISE MANAGER

Objectives

The goal of this lab is to create a linked server using Enterprise Manager.

Materials Required

This lab will require the following:

➤ Access to a computer running Windows 2000 Server, Windows 2000 Advanced Server, or Windows 2000 Datacenter Server with SQL Server 2000 installed

Estimated completion time: 20 minutes

Activity Background

The ability to create linked servers to your SQL Server is a powerful feature, allowing you to manage several servers as a group, executing commands and performing transactions on all servers at one time. These servers can be several types of relational database servers, including Microsoft SQL, Access, and Oracle. You can also link your sever to non-relational types of data stores, given that the data store has an OLE DB provider. Examples of these include Microsoft Exchange Public Mail folders and Active Directory repositories. Even though you may only have one server to work with in these labs, you still can practice the steps needed to create a linked server. If you are working in a classroom environment, or have another SQL Server available to you, replace the name NEWSQLSERVER with the name of the server available. At the end of this lab, you will view the template in Query Analyzer to add another SQL Server as a linked server using the system stored procedure sp_addlinkedserver.

ACTIVITY

1. Boot your computer and log on, if necessary.
2. Click **Start**, point to **Programs**, point to **Microsoft SQL Server**, and then click **Enterprise Manager**. The SQL Server Enterprise Manager window appears.
3. Expand **Microsoft SQL Servers**. Expand **SQL Server Group**. Expand your *server_name*.
4. Expand the **Security** folder. The four options Logins, Server Roles, Linked Servers, and Remote Servers appear under this folder.
5. Click **Linked Servers**, and then press **F1**. The SQL Server Books Online window appears.
6. Read through the displayed information titled "Configuring Linked Servers" to familiarize yourself with this functionality.
7. To close Books Online, click the **Close** button in the top-right corner of the window.
8. Right-click **Linked Servers**, and then click **New Linked Server**. The Linked Server Properties - New Linked Server dialog box opens, as shown in Figure 3-4.
9. Type the name **NEWSQLSERVER** in the Linked server text box. Under Server type, click the **SQL Server** radio button, and then click **OK**. The SQL Server Enterprise Manager dialog box opens with a message regarding the security context of the new server, and asking if you would like to continue.
10. Click **Yes**.

Lab 3.4 Creating a Linked Server Using Enterprise Manager

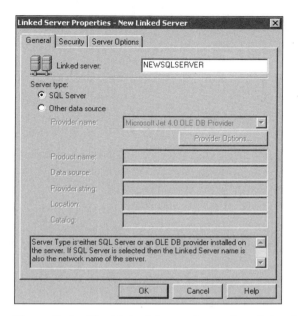

Figure 3-4 The Linked Server Properties dialog box

11. Expand **Linked Servers**, and then expand **NEWSQLSERVER**. The two options Tables and Views appear under the new linked server.

12. Click the **Tools** menu, and then click **SQL Query Analyzer**. The SQL Query Analyzer window appears.

13. If the Object Browser window is not visible, activate it by pressing **F8**.

14. Click the **Templates** tab at the bottom of the screen.

15. Expand the **Manage Linked Server** folder.

16. Double-click the **Add Sql Server as Linked Server** template. A new query window appears with the text for the T-SQL code to add another SQL Server as a linked server.

17. Click the **Window** menu, and choose the first query window. This will put the template text in the background, and return you to the blank query window where you can enter commands.

18. In the query window, type the following text:
    exec sp_addlinkedserver N'NewSQLServer2'
    go

    and then press **F5**. The message "(1 row(s) affected)" is listed twice in the Messages tab.

19. To close Query Analyzer, click the **Close** button in the top-right corner of the window. The SQL Query Analyzer dialog box opens, asking if you want to save changes.

20. Click **No To All**. You are returned to SQL Server Enterprise Manager.
21. Right-click **Linked Servers**, and then click **Refresh**. The two linked servers are displayed.
22. To close Enterprise Manager, click the **Close** button in the top-right corner of the window.

Certification Objectives

Objectives for Microsoft Exam #70-228: Installing, Configuring, and Administering Microsoft SQL Server 2000 Enterprise Edition:

➤ Create a linked server

Review Questions

1. Under what folder will you find the Linked Servers option?
   a. Databases
   b. Management
   c. Security
   d. Support Services

2. OLE DB providers exist for what type of data?
   a. Databases
   b. Text files
   c. Spreadsheet data
   d. All of the above

3. What two options appear under the linked server in Enterprise Manager?
   a. Tables and Views
   b. Diagrams and Tables
   c. Views and Stored Procedures
   d. Diagrams and Stored Procedures

4. What system stored procedure is used to list all the linked servers?
   a. sp_listlinkedservers
   b. sp_linkedservers
   c. sp_listservers
   d. sp_servers

5. What system stored procedure is used to configure a linked server?
   a. sp_linkedserverotption
   b. sp_configlinkedserver
   c. sp_serveroption
   d. sp_configserveroption

LAB 3.5 USING THE OSQL UTILITY

Objectives

The goal of this lab is to become familiar with the command prompt utility osql.

Materials Required

This lab will require the following:

➤ Access to a computer running Windows 2000 Server, Windows 2000 Advanced Server, or Windows 2000 Datacenter Server with SQL Server 2000 installed

Estimated completion time: **15 minutes**

Activity Background

According to Books Online: "The osql utility is a Microsoft Win32 command prompt utility for ad hoc, interactive execution of T-SQL statements and scripts." Basically, that means that you can use this tool similarly to the Query Analyzer, to enter T-SQL commands. In addition, you can also submit jobs by pointing to a file that contains T-SQL statements. This is particularly handy when you need to execute the same set of statements over and over again.

ACTIVITY

1. Boot your computer and log on, if necessary.

2. Click **Start**, point to **Programs**, point to **Microsoft SQL Server**, and then click **Books Online**. The SQL Server Books Online window appears.

3. In the Navigation pane, click the **Search** tab. Type **osql** in the search criteria text box, and then click **List Topics**. The results of the search are displayed.

4. Under Select topic, double-click **Using the osql Utility**. Read through the information displayed.

5. At the end of the document, under See Also, click **osql Utility**. Read through the information displayed.

6. To close Books Online, click the **Close** button in the top-right corner of the window.

7. Click **Start**, and then click **Run**. The Run dialog box opens.

8. To open a Command Prompt window, type **cmd**, and then click **OK**. The C:\WINNT\System32\cmd.exe window appears. You may also reach the command prompt by clicking **Start**, pointing to **Programs**, pointing to **Accessories**, and clicking **Command Prompt**.

Chapter 3 Administering and Configuring SQL Server 2000

9. Type **osql -?**, and then press **Enter**. The osql syntax summary is displayed.

10. Type **osql -E**, and then press **Enter**. You are connected to the default instance of SQL Server on your server, and the 1> prompt is displayed, as shown in Figure 3-5.

Figure 3-5 The osql syntax summary

Note: The -E switch is used because your server has been configured to use Windows Authentication. The -U and -P switches are used to designate a SQL Server login ID and password and require Mixed Mode authentication.

11. Type the following text at the 1> prompt, then press **Enter**:

    use pubs
    select * from authors
    go

    The contents of the authors table is displayed in the window.

12. Type **exit** at the 1> prompt. You are exited from osql, and left in a Command Prompt window.

13. Type **exit** at the C:\ prompt. The Command Prompt window is closed.

Review Questions

1. From where can osql be run?
    a. Enterprise Manager
    b. Query Analyzer
    c. Service Manager
    d. A Command Prompt window

2. Which osql switch indicates a trusted connection is to be used instead of requesting a password?
   a. -T
   b. -t
   c. -E
   d. -e

3. What is the syntax of an osql command used to connect to a named instance of a remote server?
   a. osql -S *server_name\instance_name*
   b. osql -s *server_name\instance_name*
   c. osql -S *server _name -I instance _name*
   d. osql -s *server_name -i instance_name*

4. You need to connect to a remote server on your network using osql, but you don't know the name of the server. What osql switch can you use to see a list of the servers broadcasting on your network?
   a. -l
   b. -L
   c. -n
   d. -N

5. What command is used to exit from osql?
   a. Quit
   b. Exit or Bye
   c. Quit or Exit
   d. Bye

LAB 3.6 USING THE SQLDIAG UTILITY

Objectives

The goal of this lab is to become familiar with the command prompt utility sqldiag.

Materials Required

This lab will require the following:

> ➤ Access to a computer running Windows 2000 Server, Windows 2000 Advanced Server, or Windows 2000 Datacenter Server with SQL Server 2000 installed

> Estimated completion time: **15 minutes**

Activity Background

The sqldiag utility allows you to collect and store diagnostic information about your SQL server. This information includes, but is not limited to, error logs, extended stored procedures, and configuration data. Also, if they exist, the two trace files blackbox.trc and blackbox_01.trc are copied to the output directory. These documents can then be sent to a support provider in the event of a problem with your server that cannot be resolved.

Activity

1. Boot your computer and log on, if necessary.

2. Click **Start**, point to **Programs**, point to **Microsoft SQL Server**, and then click **Books Online**. The SQL Server Books Online window appears.

3. In the Navigation pane, click the **Search** tab. Type **sqldiag** in the search criteria text box, and then click **List Topics**. The results of the search are displayed.

4. Under Select topic, double-click **sqldiag Utility**. Read through the information displayed.

5. To close Books Online, click the **Close** button in the top-right corner of the window.

6. Click **Start**, and then click **Run**. The Run dialog box opens.

7. To start a Command Prompt window, type **cmd**, and then click **OK**. The C:\WINNT\System32\cmd.exe window appears. You may also reach the command prompt by clicking **Start**, pointing to **Programs**, pointing to **Accessories**, and clicking **Command Prompt**.

8. Type the following text at the C:\ prompt:
   cd program files\Microsoft SQL Server\MSSQL\Binn
   and press **Enter**.

> Because the sqldiag utility is stored in the MSSQL\Binn directory and not in the 80\Tools\Binn directory, you must issue a cd command to change directories to the MSSQL\Binn directory before the utility can be executed.

9. Type **sqldiag -?**, and then press **Enter**. The sqldiag syntax summary is displayed.

10. Type **sqldiag**, and then press **Enter**. Several lines of information are displayed indicating that the sqldiag utility is gathering information, as shown in Figure 3-6.

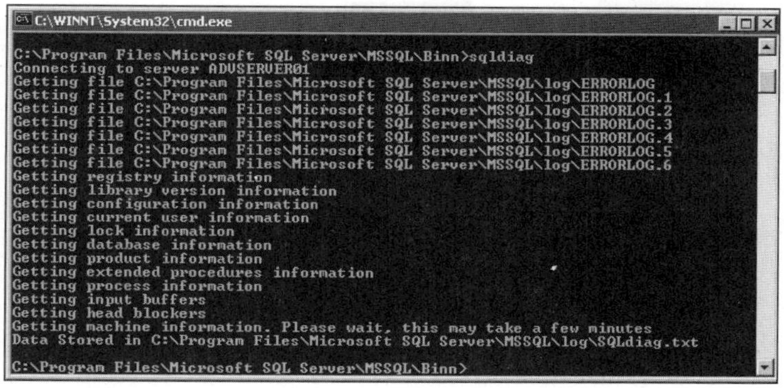

Lab 3.6 Using the Sqldiag Utility

Figure 3-6 Running the sqldiag utility

11. Type **exit** at the prompt, and then press **Enter**. The Command Prompt window is closed.

12. Click **Start**, point to **Programs**, point to **Accessories**, and then click **Windows Explorer**. The My Documents window appears.

13. Expand **My Computer**, and then expand the drive on which SQL Server is installed.

14. Expand **Program Files**, expand **Microsoft SQL Server**, and then expand **MSSQL**.

15. Click to open the **LOG** folder. The contents of the Log folder are displayed on the right.

16. Double-click the **SQLdiag** text document. The SQLdiag - Notepad window appears. Scroll to view the data in this document.

17. To close the SQLdiag window, click the **Close** button in the top-right corner of the window.

18. To close Windows Explorer, click the **Close** button in the top-right corner of the window.

Review Questions

1. From where can sqldiag be run?
   a. Enterprise Manager
   b. Query Analyzer
   c. Service Manager
   d. A Command Prompt window

2. Which sqldiag switch indicates a trusted connection is to be used instead of requesting a password?
    a. -E
    b. -e
    c. -T
    d. -t

3. What is the syntax of the sqldiag command used to connect to a named instance of SQL Server?
    a. sqldiag -S *server_name\instance_name*
    b. sqldiag -s *server_name\instance_name*
    c. sqldiag -I *instance _name*
    d. sqldiag -i *instance_name*

4. What is the default name of the output file created by the sqldiag command?
    a. Output.sql
    b. SQLdiag.txt
    c. Output.txt
    d. SQLdiag.sql

5. When can the sqldiag utility be run?
    a. Anytime
    b. When SQL Server is running
    c. When SQL Server is stopped
    d. When SQL Server is paused

CHAPTER FOUR

SQL SERVER 2000 DATABASE ARCHITECTURE

Labs included in this chapter

➤ Lab 4.1 Exploring System and User Tables Using SQL Query Analyzer
➤ Lab 4.2 Exploring System and User-Defined Data Types Using SQL Enterprise Manager
➤ Lab 4.3 Exploring Defaults and Constraints
➤ Lab 4.4 Exploring Indexes

Microsoft MCSE Exam #70-228 Objectives	
Objective	Lab
Create and manage objects, including constraints, indexes, stored procedures, triggers, and views	4.1, 4.2, 4.3, 4.4

LAB 4.1 EXPLORING SYSTEM AND USER TABLES USING SQL QUERY ANALYZER

Objectives

The goal of this lab is to become familiar with the system and user tables that comprise a user database.

Materials Required

This lab will require the following:

> ➤ Access to a computer running Windows 2000 Server, Windows 2000 Advanced Server, or Windows 2000 Datacenter Server with SQL Server 2000 installed

> ➤ Familiarity with SQL Query Analyzer (obtained in Lab 3.2)

Estimated completion time: **15 minutes**

Activity Background

Besides Registry settings, SQL Server 2000 uses a series of tables to store all the information it needs to do its job. Some of these tables are in a database called master, which we will examine in more detail in Chapter 5. Other tables are duplicated in every user database. In this lab, you will use Query Analyzer to look at both the system and user tables contained in the Northwind database.

ACTIVITY

1. Boot your computer, and log on by pressing **Ctrl+Alt+Del**. In the Log On to Windows window, type your user name and password in the text boxes, and then press **Enter**. The Windows 2000 desktop appears on your screen.

2. Click **Start**, point to **Programs**, point to **Microsoft SQL Server**, and then click **Query Analyzer**. The Connect to SQL Server dialog box opens.

3. Verify that **(local)** is listed in the SQL Server text box and that the **Windows authentication** radio button is selected, and then click **OK**. The SQL Query Analyzer window appears.

4. If the Object Browser window is not visible, activate it by pressing **F8**.

5. Expand the **Northwind** database. Expand the **User Tables** folder. The user tables are listed.

6. Expand **System Tables**. The 19 system tables are listed.

Lab 4.1 Exploring System and User Tables Using SQL Query Analyzer 65

 The database engine uses these 19 system tables to define the Northwind database and many things relating to it. Notice there is no systables table. This is because tables are objects, and the sysobjects table tracks all objects.

7. Right-click the **dbo.sysobjects** table, and then click **Open**. The contents of the sysobjects table are displayed on the right side of the screen. Scroll down and over to view the entire contents.

8. Click the **Window** menu, and then click **Query**. The Open Table window is put in the background, and you are returned to the query window where T-SQL commands can be entered and executed.

9. Type the following text in the query window:

   use northwind
   select * from sysobjects
   where type = 'u'
   order by name
   go

   and then press F5. The results of this select statement are displayed in the bottom half of the query window, as shown in Figure 4-1.

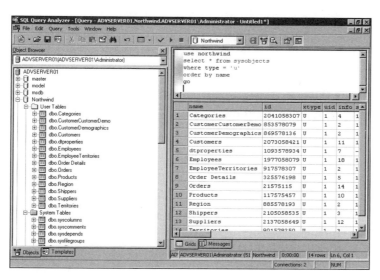

Figure 4-1   Querying the dbo.sysobjects table

10. The results of this query should match the list of User Tables in the Object Browser window.

11. In the query, change the type from **u** to **s**, and re-execute the query. The results of this select statement are displayed in the bottom half of the query window.

12. Compare the results of this query with the list of System Tables in the Object Browser window.

13. To close Query Analyzer, click the **Close** button in the top-right corner of the window. The SQL Query Analyzer dialog box opens, asking if you want to save changes.
14. Click **No To All**.

Certification Objectives

Objectives for Microsoft Exam #70-228: Installing, Configuring, and Administering Microsoft SQL Server 2000 Enterprise Edition:

➤ Create and manage objects, including constraints, indexes, stored procedures, triggers, and views

Review Questions

1. Which system table contains the list of the user tables for a database?
   a. systables
   b. sysusertables
   c. sysobjects
   d. sysuserobjects

2. What T-SQL command indicates the database against which to execute commands?
   a. USE
   b. DATABASE
   c. USEDATABASE
   d. DATABASEUSED

3. What does the asterisk (*) in the T-SQL command *select * from sysobjects* indicate?
   a. All rows
   b. All columns
   c. The * row
   d. The * column

4. Which of the following is not true of a system table?
   a. The name contains the "sys" prefix
   b. It has a type of 's'
   c. It has an xtype of 's'
   d. The name is always plural

5. How many system tables are created for every user database?
   a. 10
   b. 14
   c. 19
   d. 50

Lab 4.2 Exploring System and User-Defined Data Types Using SQL Enterprise Manager

Objectives

The goal of this lab is to become familiar with the system data types supplied with SQL Server 2000, and then explore how user-defined data types are created based on a system data type.

Materials Required

This lab will require the following:

➤ Access to a computer running Windows 2000 Server, Windows 2000 Advanced Server, or Windows 2000 Datacenter Server with SQL Server 2000 installed

Estimated completion time: **20 minutes**

Activity Background

According to Books Online, a data type "defines the type of data a column can hold," and a user-defined data type "makes a table structure more meaningful to programmers and helps ensure that columns holding similar classes of data have the same base data type." In this lab, you will use Enterprise Manager to view the system supplied data types, and then look at one particular user-defined data type defined in the pubs database.

Activity

1. Boot your computer and log on, if necessary.

2. Click **Start**, point to **Programs**, point to **Microsoft SQL Server**, and then click **Enterprise Manager**. The SQL Server Enterprise Manager window appears.

3. Expand **Microsoft SQL Servers**, expand **SQL Server Group**, and then expand your *server_name*.

4. Expand **Databases**, and then expand the **pubs** database. Click **Tables**. The list of both user and system tables is displayed.

5. In the Tables list, right-click **systypes**, point to **Open Table**, and then click **Return all rows**. The 29 system supplied data types are displayed, as shown in Figure 4-2. Maximize the window, if necessary, to view all data.

68   Chapter 4   SQL Server 2000 Database Architecture

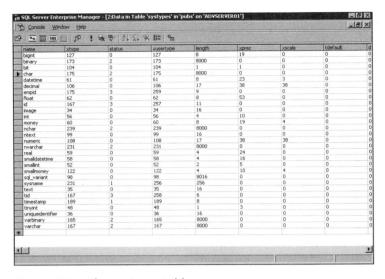

Figure 4-2   The systypes table

6. Read through the information stored in this table, taking specific notice of the char data type.

7. Click the **Window** menu, and then click **Console Root**. You are returned to the SQL Server Enterprise Manager window.

8. In the Tree pane, under the pubs database, click **User Defined Data Types**. The three user-defined data types (empid, id, and tid) are displayed.

9. Right-click **empid**, and then click **Properties**. The User-Defined Data Type Properties dialog box opens, as shown in Figure 4-3.

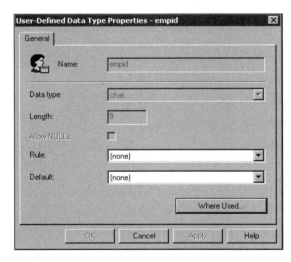

Figure 4-3   The User-Defined Data Type Properties dialog box

Lab 4.2 Exploring System and User-Defined Data Types Using SQL Enterprise Manager 69

 The empid user-defined data type is based on the char system data type, but is restricted to only nine characters in length. This data type could be used to enforce a business rule, or perhaps to limit data entry when new records are created.

10. Click the **Where Used** button. The Where Used dialog box opens.
11. Notice that the empid user-defined data type is used in the employee table on the emp_id field.
12. Click **Cancel** twice to close the Where Used and the User-Defined Data Type Properties dialog boxes.
13. In the tree pane, under the pubs database, click **Tables**. The list of both user and system tables is displayed.
14. In the Tables list, double-click the **employee** table. The Table Properties dialog box opens, as shown in Figure 4-4.

Figure 4-4 Viewing the empid user-defined data type in the Table Properties - employee dialog box

15. Notice the emp_id field has the empid data type.
16. Click **Cancel** to close the Table Properties dialog box.
17. To close Enterprise Manager, click the **Close** button in the top-right corner of the window.

Certification Objectives

Objectives for Microsoft Exam #70-228: Installing, Configuring, and Administering Microsoft SQL Server 2000 Enterprise Edition:

➤ Create and manage objects, including constraints, indexes, stored procedures, triggers, and views

Review Questions

1. Which system table contains the list of the system supplied data types for a database?
   a. systypes
   b. syssystemtypes
   c. sysobjects
   d. syssystemobjects

2. What is the maximum length of a column with the char data type?
   a. 256
   b. 800
   c. 8000
   d. 8016

3. What are user-defined data types based on?
   a. A length
   b. A rule
   c. A default
   d. A system supplied data type

4. A user-defined data type can have a _____ defined.
   a. rule
   b. default
   c. rule and a default
   d. rule or a default

5. Where can a user-defined data type be used?
   a. Across all databases on a server
   b. In the database where it is defined only
   c. In the table where it is defined only
   d. On the column where it is defined only

Lab 4.3 Exploring Defaults and Constraints

Objectives

The goal of this lab is to become familiar with defaults and constraints by looking at examples of both in the pubs database.

Materials Required

This lab will require the following:

➤ Access to a computer running Windows 2000 Server, Windows 2000 Advanced Server, or Windows 2000 Datacenter Server with SQL Server 2000 installed

Est mated completion time: **20 minutes**

Activity Background

Defaults and constraints help to define your database and ensure that the users who are entering data into your database do so in a consistent manner. A default can be defined as a unique object, given a name, and be reused throughout a database, or can be implemented on a particular column in the form of a default constraint. There are several types of constraints other than default constraints, including primary key, foreign key, and check constraints. In this lab, you will look at some of the constraints defined in the pubs database using both Enterprise Manager and Query Analyzer.

Activity

1. Boot your computer and log on, if necessary.

2. Click **Start**, point to **Programs**, point to **Microsoft SQL Server**, and then click **Enterprise Manager**. The SQL Server Enterprise Manager window appears.

3. Expand **Microsoft SQL Servers**, expand **SQL Server Group**, and then expand your *server_name*.

4. Expand **Databases**, and then expand the **pubs** database. Click **Defaults**. Notice that there are no defaults defined for this database.

5. Press **F1** to evoke Books Online. Read the document titled "Defaults."

6. To close Books Online, click the **Close** button in the top-right corner of the window. You are returned to the SQL Server Enterprise Manager window.

7. Click **Tables**. The list of both system and user tables defined for this database is displayed on the right side of the window.

8. Double-click the **authors** table. The Table Properties dialog box opens, as shown in Figure 4-5.

The key graphic associated with the au_id column indicates that there is a primary key constraint on the au_id column; the default 'UNKNOWN' associated with the phone column indicates that there is a default constraint on the phone column.

Figure 4-5 The Table Properties dialog box for the authors table

9. Click **Cancel** to close the Table Properties dialog box.
10. Click the **Tools** menu, and then click **SQL Query Analyzer**. The SQL Query Analyzer window appears.
11. If the Object Browser window is not visible, activate it by pressing **F5**.
12. In the Object Browser window, expand the **pubs** database, expand the **User Tables** folder, and then expand the **dbo.authors** table. Five folders (Columns, Indexes, Constraints, Dependencies, and Triggers) appear under this database.
13. Expand **Constraints**. The four constraints defined for this table are displayed. Notice the primary key and default constraints (that you viewed using Enterprise Manager) are listed, as well as two additional constraints.
14. One at a time, right-click each of the two check constraints, point to **Script Object to New Window As**, and then click **Create**. The T-SQL code used to create each constraint is displayed in a query window, as shown in Figure 4-6. Scroll to read the entire line of code for each statement.

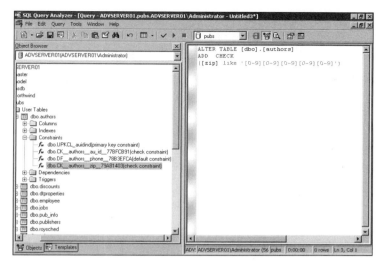

Figure 4-6 Viewing the T-SQL code to create the check constraint defined in the zip column in the authors table

15. To close Query Analyzer, click the **Close** button in the top-right corner of the window. The SQL Query Analyzer dialog box opens, asking if you want to save changes.

16. Click **No To All**. You are returned to Enterprise Manager.

17. To close Enterprise Manager, click the **Close** button in the top-right corner of the window.

Certification Objectives

Objectives for Microsoft Exam #70-228: Installing, Configuring, and Administering Microsoft SQL Server 2000 Enterprise Edition:

➤ Create and manage objects, including constraints, indexes, stored procedures, triggers, and views

Review Questions

1. Which of the following cannot be defined as a default?
    a. Constant
    b. Variable
    c. Mathematical expression
    d. Built-in function

2. What is the preferred standard method to apply a default?
   a. Create a default object using the CREATE DEFAULT statement.
   b. Create a default object using Enterprise Manager.
   c. Create a default object using Query Analyzer.
   d. Create a default definition using the DEFAULT keyword in the CREATE TABLE statement.

3. What graphical symbol indicates that a primary key constraint has been placed on a column (as viewed through Enterprise Manager)?
   a. A key
   b. A lock
   c. P
   d. PK

4. What T-SQL statement, used to add a check constraint to an existing table, begins with the following code?
   a. ALTER TABLE *table_name* add check…
   b. ADD CHECK to table *table_name*…
   c. ALTER TABLE Add Check to *table_name*…
   d. ADD CHECK to *table_name* table…

5. What T-SQL statement, used to add a default constraint to an existing table, begins with the following code?
   a. ALTER TABLE *table_name* add default…
   b. ADD DEFAULT to table *table_name*…
   c. ALTER TABLE *table_name* add constraint…
   d. ADD DEFAULT to *table_name* table….

LAB 4.4 EXPLORING INDEXES

Objectives

The goal of this lab is to become familiar with three different types of indexes: clustered, nonclustered, and composite.

Materials Required

This lab will require the following:

> ➤ Access to a computer running Windows 2000 Server, Windows 2000 Advanced Server, or Windows 2000 Datacenter Server with SQL Server 2000 installed

Lab 4.4 Exploring Indexes

Estimated completion time: **30 minutes**

Activity Background

Indexes, if placed and maintained properly throughout your database, can make or break the database's performance. SQL Server 2000 sometimes creates indexes for you, in the case of a primary key or unique constraint. Other times, you, as the database administrator, will create indexes to speed up the extraction of data from your database. In this lab, you will look at the indexes that are part of the pubs database and view the T-SQL code used to create them.

Activity

1. Boot your computer and log on, if necessary.

2. Click **Start**, point to **Programs**, point to **Microsoft SQL Server**, and then click **Query Analyzer**. The Connect to SQL Server window appears.

3. Verify that **(local)** is listed in the SQL Server text box, and that the **Windows authentication** radio button is selected, and then click **OK**. The SQL Query Analyzer window appears.

4. Press **F1** to evoke Books Online.

5. In the Navigation pane, click the **Search** tab. Type **"creating an index"** (including the quotes) in the search criteria text box, and then click **List Topics**. The results of the search are displayed.

6. Under Select topic, double-click **Creating an Index** (in the location Creating and Maintaining Databases). Read through the information titled "Creating an Index."

7. To close Books Online, click the **Close** button in the top-right corner of the window. You are returned to the SQL Query Analyzer window.

8. If the Object Browser window is not visible, activate it by pressing **F8**.

9. Expand the **pubs** database, expand the **User Tables** folder, and then expand the **dbo.employee** table. Five folders are displayed: Columns, Indexes, Constraints, Dependencies, and Triggers.

10. Expand **Indexes**. The index employee_ind is displayed.

11. Right-click the **employee_ind** index, point to **Script Object to New Window As**, and then click **Create**. The T-SQL code used to create this index is displayed in a query window, as shown in Figure 4-7. Scroll to read the entire line of code for this statement.

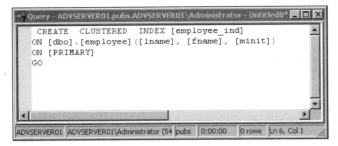

Figure 4-7 Viewing the code to create a clustered index

12. Expand the **dbo.sales** table. Five folders are displayed: Columns, Indexes, Constraints, Dependencies, and Triggers.

13. Expand **Indexes**. The index titleidind is displayed.

14. Right-click the **titleidind** index, point to **Script Object to New Window As**, and then click **Create**. The T-SQL code used to create this index is displayed in a query window, as shown in Figure 4-8. Scroll to read the entire line of code for this statement.

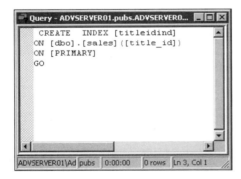

Figure 4-8 Viewing the code to create a nonclustered index

15. Expand the **dbo.authors** table. Five folders are displayed: Columns, Indexes, Constraints, Dependencies, and Triggers.

16. Expand **Indexes**. The index aunmind is displayed.

17. Right-click the **aunmind** index, point to **Script Object to New Window As**, and then click **Create**. The T-SQL code used to create this index is displayed in a query window, as shown in Figure 4-9. Scroll to read the entire line of code for this statement.

 This index is defined for two columns. This is known as a composite index.

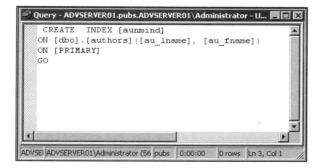

Figure 4-9 Viewing the code to create a composite index

18. To close SQL Query Analyzer, click the **Close** button in the top-right corner of the window. The SQL Query Analyzer dialog box opens, asking if you want to save changes.

19. Click **No To All**.

Certification Objectives

Objectives for Microsoft Exam #70-228: Installing, Configuring, and Administering Microsoft SQL Server 2000 Enterprise Edition:

➤ Create and manage objects, including constraints, indexes, stored procedures, triggers, and views

Review Questions

1. Microsoft SQL Server 2000 automatically creates unique indexes to enforce the uniqueness requirements of what type of constraints?
    a. Primary Key
    b. Foreign Key
    c. Unique
    d. Primary Key and Unique

2. What is the maximum number of nonclustered indexes that can be created on a table?
    a. 249
    b. 250
    c. 255
    d. 256

3. What is the maximum number of columns that can be used to create a composite index?
    a. 8
    b. 10
    c. 16
    d. 24

4. What simultaneous operation will block the creation of an index?
    a. Adding records to the table
    b. Adding tables to the database
    c. Selecting records from the table
    d. Backing up the database

5. What is the preferred method of building indexes on a large table?
    a. Build the nonclustered indexes first, and then build the clustered index.
    b. Build the clustered index, and then build the nonclustered index.
    c. Drop the nonclustered indexes first, and then drop the clustered index.
    d. Drop the clustered index, and then drop the nonclustered index.

CHAPTER FIVE

CREATING SQL SERVER 2000 DATABASES

Labs included in this chapter

- Lab 5.1 Exploring the System Databases
- Lab 5.2 Creating a Database
- Lab 5.3 Expanding and Shrinking a Database
- Lab 5.4 Changing Database Options; Renaming and Deleting Databases
- Lab 5.5 Creating Tables in a Database
- Lab 5.6 Creating a Foreign Key Relationship

Microsoft MCSE Exam #70-228 Objectives	
Objective	Lab
Create and alter databases	5.2, 5.4
Add filegroups, configure filegroup usage	5.4
Expand and shrink a database	5.3
Set database options by using the ALTER DATABASE or CREATE DATABASE statements	5.4

LAB 5.1 EXPLORING THE SYSTEM DATABASES

Objectives

The goal of this lab is to become familiar with the system databases and the T-SQL system stored procedure sp_helpdb.

Materials Required

This lab will require the following:

➤ Access to a computer running Windows 2000 Server, Windows 2000 Advanced Server, or Windows 2000 Datacenter Server with SQL Server 2000 installed

➤ Familiarity with Query Analyzer (obtained in Lab 3.2)

Estimated completion time: **10 minutes**

Activity Background

The system databases are created during the installation of SQL Server 2000 and are used by the server itself to do its job. The master database is the most important database on your server because is contains information about all the other system databases as well as all user databases. In this lab, you will use the system stored procedure sp_helpdb to gather information about the system databases.

Activity

1. Boot your computer, and log on by pressing **Ctrl+Alt+Del**. In the Log On to Windows window, type your user name and password in the text boxes, and then press **Enter**. The Windows 2000 desktop appears on your screen.

2. Click **Start**, point to **Programs**, point to **Microsoft SQL Server**, and then click **Query Analyzer**. The Connect to SQL Server dialog box opens.

3. Verify that **(local)** is listed in the SQL Server text box, and that the **Windows authentication** radio button is selected, and then click **OK**. The SQL Query Analyzer window appears.

4. In the query window, type the following text:

   sp_helpdb

   and execute the command by pressing **F5**. The results of the command are displayed in the bottom section of the window.

5. Scroll over to read the entire result.

6. In the query window, change the text to read:

   sp_helpdb master

   and execute the command by pressing **F5**. The results of the command are displayed in the bottom section of the window.

7. If necessary, scroll over to read the entire result.

8. Repeat Steps 6 and 7, replacing master with the name of each of the system and sample databases (as listed in the results of Step 4).

9. To close Query Analyzer, click the **Close** button in the top-right corner of the window. The SQL Query Analyzer dialog box opens, asking if you want to save changes.

10. Click **No To All**.

Review Questions

1. Which database is re-created each time the server is booted?
   a. Master
   b. Model
   c. Msdb
   d. Tempdb

2. The system databases are stored in what filegroup?
   a. Primary
   b. Null
   c. Secondary
   d. Default

3. What three-letter extension is used for the primary data file for a database?
   a. .kdf
   b. .ldf
   c. .mdf
   d. .ndf

4. What three-letter extension is used for the log file for a database?
   a. .kdf
   b. .ldf
   c. .mdf
   d. .ndf

5. What object is never stored in a filegroup?
   a. The primary data file
   b. The secondary data file
   c. The log file
   d. An index

Lab 5.2 Creating a Database

Objectives

The goal of this lab is to become familiar with how to create a database, using both Enterprise Manager and T-SQL code.

Materials Required

This lab will require the following:

➤ Access to a computer running Windows 2000 Server, Windows 2000 Advanced Server, or Windows 2000 Datacenter Server with SQL Server 2000 installed

Estimated completion time: **20 minutes**

Activity Background

After you install and configure your SQL server, the next step is to create user databases. This step must, of course, be taken as you are setting up a new SQL server, but may also need to be done throughout its use. Databases may need to be created for new data generated by a growing company or for testing purposes. In this lab, you will create a database using Enterprise Manager and then create two databases using T-SQL code.

Activity

To create a database using Enterprise Manager:

1. Boot your computer and log on, if necessary.

2. Click **Start**, point to **Programs**, point to **Microsoft SQL Server**, and then click **Enterprise Manager**. The SQL Server Enterprise Manager window appears.

3. Expand **Microsoft SQL Servers**, expand **SQL Server Group**, and then expand your *server_name*.

4. Click **Databases**. Click the **Action** menu, and then click **New Database**. The Database Properties dialog box opens.

5. On the General tab in the Name text box, type **CompanyONE**.

6. Click the **Data Files** tab. Click the **ellipses** button (under Location). The Locate Database File dialog box opens.

7. Notice the default location and name of the data file for your new database. Click **Cancel** to close the Locate Database File dialog box.

8. Under File properties, change the File growth option from **By percent** to **In megabytes**, and the Restrict file growth (MB) option to 200 MBs, as shown in Figure 5-1.

Figure 5-1 Setting file properties in the Database Properties dialog box

 The settings just chosen are for demonstration purposes only. If a database is unrestricted, it could fill the entire disk, and could halt all other activities depending on that disk. Alternately, if restricted and the maximum is met, no additional data can be added to or changed in the database, and user activity is impeded. Also, a file growth of 1 MB is usually too small for a large production database, but could be just right for a small database that experiences few changes. Only thorough research into your database's activity will determine the proper settings.

9. Click the **Transaction Log** tab. Click the **ellipses** button (under Location). The Locate Transaction Log File dialog box opens.

10. Notice the default location and name of the transaction log file for your new database. Click **Cancel** to close the Locate Transaction Log File dialog box.

11. Under File properties, change the File growth option from **By percent** to **In megabytes**, but leave the Maximum file size option unrestricted.

12. Click **OK** to complete the creation of your new database.
13. To close Enterprise Manager, click the **Close** button in the top-right corner of the window.

To view the files created by Enterprise Manager:

1. Click **Start**, point to **Programs**, point to **Accessories**, and then click **Windows Explorer**. The My Documents window appears.
2. Expand **My Computer**, and then expand the drive on which SQL Server is installed.
3. Expand **Program Files**, expand **Microsoft SQL Server**, and then expand **MSSQL**.
4. Click to open the **Data** folder. The contents of the Data folder are displayed on the right. Notice the CompanyONE_Data and CompanyONE_Log files.
5. To minimize Windows Explorer, click the **Minimize** button in the top-right corner of the window.

To create databases using T-SQL code:

1. Click **Start**, point to **Programs**, point to **Microsoft SQL Server**, and then click **Query Analyzer**. The Connect to SQL Server dialog box opens.
2. Verify that **(local)** is listed in the SQL Server text box, and that the **Windows authentication** radio button is selected, and then click **OK**. The SQL Query Analyzer window appears.
3. At the bottom of the Object Browser window, click the **Templates** tab.
4. Expand **Create Database**, and then double-click **Create Database Basic Template**. Notice the simple CREATE DATABASE statement.
5. Click the **Window** menu, and then click the first query window.
6. In the query window, type the following text:

   use master
   go
   create database CompanyTWO
   go

   and then execute the query by pressing **F5**. Two messages appear in the bottom section of the query window indicating that the data and log files were created, as shown in Figure 5-2.

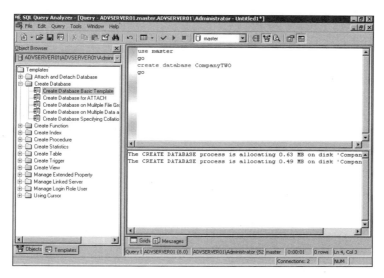

Figure 5-2 Creating a database using T-SQL code

7. Return to Windows Explorer, and then refresh the contents of the Data folder by clicking the **View** menu and then clicking **Refresh**. Notice the difference in the naming convention used with the databases.

8. Return to Query Analyzer, and then double-click **Create Database on Multiple Data and Transaction Log Files**. Notice the complex CREATE DATABASE statement.

9. Click the **Window** menu, and then click the first query window.

10. In the query window, delete the previous text, and then type the following text:
    **use master
    go
    Create database Company3
    ON Primary
    (name = Company3DATA,
    filename = 'c:\program files\Microsoft SQL
            Server\mssql\Data\Company3DATA.mdf',
    size = 10MB,
    maxsize = 200MB,
    filegrowth = 10%)
    Log ON
    (name = Company3LOG,
    filename = 'c:\program files\Microsoft SQL
            Server\mssql\Data\Company3LOG.ldf',
    size = 5MB,
    maxsize = 200MB,
    filegrowth = 10%)
    go**

Execute the query by pressing F5. Two messages appear in the bottom section of the query window indicating that the data and log files were created.

11. Return to Windows Explorer, and then refresh the contents of the Data folder by clicking the **View** menu and then clicking **Refresh**. Notice the difference in the naming convention used with the databases.

12. To close Windows Explorer, click the **Close** button in the top-right corner of the window.

13. To close Query Analyzer, click the **Close** button in the top-right corner of the window. The SQL Query Analyzer dialog box opens, asking if you want to save changes.

14. Click **No To All**.

Certification Objectives

Objectives for Microsoft Exam #70-228: Installing, Configuring, and Administering Microsoft SQL Server 2000 Enterprise Edition:

➤ Create and alter databases

Review Questions

1. Using Enterprise Manager, what is the default filename of the primary data file for a new database named TEST?
   a. TEST.mdf
   b. TEST.ndf
   c. TEST_Data.mdf
   d. TEST_Data.ndf

2. Using Enterprise Manager, what is the default file growth for both the data file and the transaction log file?
   a. 1 MB
   b. 10 MB
   c. 1 percent
   d. 10 percent

3. In the T-SQL code used to create a database, what information should not be included in the parentheses?
   a. Database name
   b. Logical file name
   c. Size
   d. Maxsize

4. What punctuation mark separates the parameters within the parentheses of the T-SQL code used to create a database?
   a. Space
   b. Comma
   c. Semicolon
   d. Colon

5. What command should be issued before the CREATE DATABASE statement (to ensure you are "in" the proper database)?
   a. MASTER
   b. IN MASTER
   c. USE MASTER
   d. CURRENT MASTER

LAB 5.3 EXPANDING AND SHRINKING A DATABASE

Objectives

The goal of this lab is to become familiar with how to expand and shrink a database, using both Enterprise Manager and T-SQL code.

Materials Required

This lab will require the following:

➤ Access to a computer running Windows 2000 Server, Windows 2000 Advanced Server, or Windows 2000 Datacenter Server with SQL Server 2000 installed

➤ The CompanyTWO and Company3 databases (created in Lab 5.2)

Estimated completion time: **20 minutes**

Activity Background

Expanding and shrinking a database is a major part of any SQL Server administrator's job. There must always be space to insert and update records in the data files, and if the transaction log becomes full, all activity on that database halts. You can use either Enterprise Manager or T-SQL code to easily expand a database (and/or its files). You can use Enterprise Manager or a Database Console Command (DBCC) to shrink a database.

ACTIVITY

To expand a database using Enterprise Manager:

1. Boot your computer and log on, if necessary.

2. Click **Start**, point to **Programs**, point to **Microsoft SQL Server**, and then click **Enterprise Manager**. The SQL Server Enterprise Manager window appears.

3. Expand **Microsoft SQL Servers**, expand **SQL Server Group**, and then expand your *server_name*.

4. Expand **Databases**. Right-click the **CompanyTWO** database, and then click **Properties**. The CompanyTWO Properties dialog box opens.

5. Click the **Data Files** tab. Click in the Space allocated (MB) box, and change the value from **1** to **10**.

6. Click the **Transaction Log** tab. Click in the Space allocated (MB) box, and change the value from **1** to **5**, as shown in Figure 5-3.

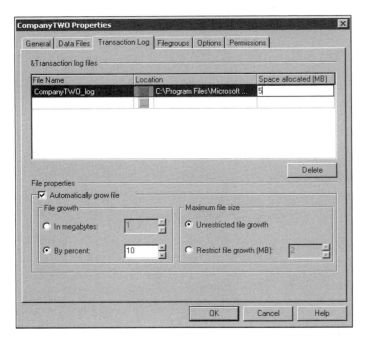

Figure 5-3 Expanding the size of the transaction log file

7. Click **OK** to complete the expansion of the data file.

To verify the file size changes:

1. Click **Start**, point to **Programs**, point to **Accessories**, and then click **Windows Explorer**. The My Documents window appears.

2. Expand **My Computer**, and then expand the drive on which SQL Server is installed.

3. Expand **Program Files**, expand **Microsoft SQL Server**, and then expand **MSSQL**.

4. Click to open the **Data** folder. The contents of the data folder are displayed on the right. Notice the new size of the CompanyTWO and CompanyTWO_log files.

5. To minimize Windows Explorer, click the **Minimize** button in the top-right corner of the window.

To expand a database using T-SQL code:

1. Click **Start**, point to **Programs**, point to **Microsoft SQL Server**, and then click **Query Analyzer**. The Connect to SQL Server dialog box opens.

2. Verify that **(local)** is listed in the SQL Server text box, and that the **Windows authentication** radio button is selected, and then click **OK**. The SQL Query Analyzer window appears.

3. In the query window, type the following text:

   use master
   go
   Alter database CompanyTWO Modify File
   (name = CompanyTWO, size = 100)
   Alter database CompanyTWO Modify File
   (name = CompanyTWO_log, size = 50)
   go

   and then execute the query by pressing **F5**. A message appears in the bottom section of the query window indicating that the commands completed successfully, as shown in Figure 5-4.

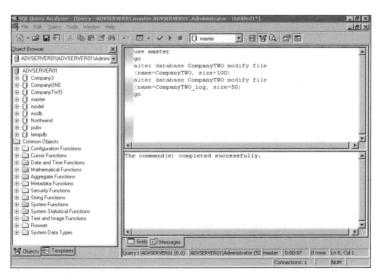

Figure 5-4 Expanding the size of the data and transaction log files

4. Return to Windows Explorer, and then refresh the contents of the Data folder by clicking the **View** menu and then clicking **Refresh**. Notice the difference in the naming convention used with the databases.

5. To minimize Windows Explorer, click the **Minimize** button in the top-right corner of the window.

6. To minimize Query Analyzer, click the **Minimize** button in the top-right corner of the window. You are returned to Enterprise Manager.

To shrink a database using Enterprise Manager:

1. Right-click the **CompanyTWO** database, point to **All Tasks**, and then click **Shrink Database**. The Shrink Database dialog box opens, as shown in Figure 5-5.

Figure 5-5 The Shrink Database dialog box

2. Under Shrink action, in the Maximum free space in files after shrinking box, type **25**, and then click **OK**. The SQL Server Enterprise Manager dialog box opens indicating that the database has been shrunk successfully. Click **OK**.

 A database cannot be shrunk smaller than its original size. For example, if a database is created with an original size of 100 MBs, and the data entered only requires 50 MBs, the database cannot be shrunk. In contrast, database *files* can be shrunk smaller than their original size using the DBCC SHRINKFILE command.

3. Return to Windows Explorer, and then refresh the contents of the Data folder by clicking the **View** menu and then clicking **Refresh**. Notice the difference in the size of the CompanyTWO and CompanyTWO_log files.

4. To minimize Windows Explorer, click the **Minimize** button in the top-right corner of the window.

To shrink a database using the DBCC command:

1. Return to Query Analyzer. Delete the previous text in the query window, and then type the following text:

   **use Company3
   go
   dbcc shrinkfile('company3data',5)
   go
   dbcc shrinkfile('company3log',3)
   go**

   Execute the query by pressing **F5**. Two grids appear in the bottom section of the query window.

2. Return to Windows Explorer, and then refresh the contents of the Data folder by clicking the **View** menu and then clicking **Refresh**. Notice the difference in the size of the Company3DATA and Company3_log files.

3. To close Windows Explorer, click the **Close** button in the top-right corner of the window.

4. To close Query Analyzer, click the **Close** button in the top-right corner of the window. The SQL Query Analyzer dialog box opens, asking if you want to save changes.

5. Click **No To All**. You are returned to Enterprise Manager.

6. To close Enterprise Manager, click the **Close** button in the top-right corner of the window.

Certification Objectives

Objectives for Microsoft Exam #70-228: Installing, Configuring, and Administering Microsoft SQL Server 2000 Enterprise Edition:

➤ Expand and shrink a database

Review Questions

1. Using Enterprise Manager, in the *database_name* Properties dialog box, what option should you use to prevent a file from growing until disk space is exhausted?
   a. Unrestricted file growth
   b. Restrict file growth (MB)
   c. Filegrowth =
   d. Maxsize =

2. What T-SQL statement is used to expand a data or log file of a database?
   a. EXPAND DATABASE *database_name*
   b. ALTER DATABASE *database_name* Increase File
   c. ALTER DATABASE *database_name* Modify File
   d. EXPAND DATABASE *database_name* Modify File

3. What can you shrink using Enterprise Manager?
   a. The entire database
   b. The data file only
   c. The log file only
   d. All of the above

4. In the command DBCC SHRINKFILE('*datafilename*',X), what does X represent?
   a. The desired size of the data file after the command is executed, in MB
   b. The desired size of the data file after the command is executed, in KB
   c. The amount of space by which to reduce the data file, in MB
   d. The amount of space by which to reduce the data file, in KB

5. What option can be used on the DBCC SHRINKFILE command to shrink the file to the last allocated extent, but does not move any data?
   a. NOTRUNCATE
   b. TRUNCATE ONLY
   c. EMPTYFILE
   d. RELEASE

LAB 5.4 CHANGING DATABASE OPTIONS; RENAMING AND DELETING DATABASES

Objectives

The goal of this lab is to become familiar with how to change a database's options, rename a database, and delete a database.

Materials Required

This lab will require the following:

➤ Access to a computer running Windows 2000 Server, Windows 2000 Advanced Server, or Windows 2000 Datacenter Server with SQL Server 2000 installed

➤ The CompanyTWO and Company3 databases (created in Lab 5.2)

Lab 5.4 Changing Database Options; Renaming and Deleting Databases

Estimated completion time: **20 minutes**

Activity Background

After a database has been created, you may need to change one or more of the options for that database. In Chapter 3, you learned how to set options for an entire server. Those options affect all databases on the server. In this chapter, you will set options that affect only a single database. Some options can be set using Enterprise Manager, while others must be set using the T-SQL command ALTER DATABASE. The sp_dboption system stored procedure is also available for use, but is mainly supplied for backward compatibility, and will most likely not be available in future releases of SQL Server. In this lab, you will set the Auto shrink option for a database, create a new filegroup, and create a new data file on that new filegroup using Enterprise Manager. You will also set the Auto shrink option for a database using T-SQL code. Next, you will rename a database and see how the changed database name does not affect the data and log filenames. Finally, you will delete two databases, one with Enterprise Manager and one with the T-SQL command DROP DATABASE.

Activity

To set the Auto shrink option, and create a new filegroup and new data file within that filegroup:

1. Boot your computer and log on, if necessary.

2. Click **Start**, point to **Programs**, point to **Microsoft SQL Server**, and then click **Enterprise Manager**. The SQL Server Enterprise Manager window appears.

3. Expand **Microsoft SQL Servers**, expand **SQL Server Group**, expand your *server_name*, and then expand **Databases**.

4. Right-click the **CompanyTWO** database, and then click **Properties**. The CompanyTWO Properties dialog box opens.

5. Click the **Options** tab, and then click the **Auto shrink** check box, as shown in Figure 5-6.

Chapter 5 Creating SQL Server 2000 Databases

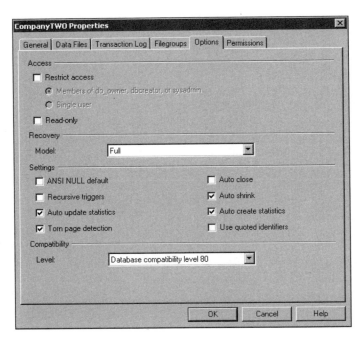

Figure 5-6 Setting the Auto shrink option for a database using Enterprise Manager

 Remember, when a database is created, the model database is copied, and all database settings are inherited from model.

6. Click the **Filegroups** tab. Click to set the cursor in the Name box (under PRIMARY), type **NEWFILEGROUP**, and then click **OK**.

7. Right-click the **CompanyTWO** database, and then click **Properties**. The CompanyTWO Properties dialog box opens.

8. Click the **Data Files** Tab. Click to set the cursor in the File Name box (under CompanyTWO), and type **Co_TWO_NFG**. Click under Filegroup (where it currently reads PRIMARY), and a list arrow appears. Click the list arrow, and then click **NEWFILEGROUP**, as shown in Figure 5-7.

Lab 5.4 Changing Database Options; Renaming and Deleting Databases

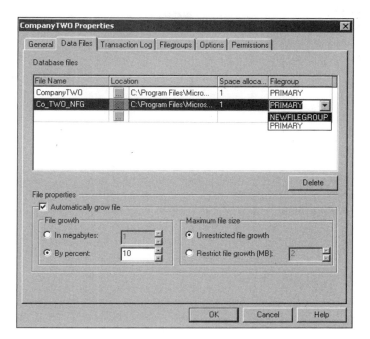

Figure 5-7 Creating a new database file on a new filegroup

9. Click **OK** to complete the creation of the new database file on the new filegroup.

To view the newly created file in the file list:

1. Click **Start**, point to **Programs**, point to **Accessories**, and then click **Windows Explorer**. The My Documents window appears.

2. Expand **My Computer**, and then expand the drive on which SQL Server is installed.

3. Expand **Program Files**, expand **Microsoft SQL Server**, and then expand **MSSQL**.

4. Click to open the **Data** folder. The contents of the data folder are displayed on the right. Notice the new Co_TWO_NFG_Data.NDF file.

5. To minimize Windows Explorer, click the **Minimize** button in the top-right corner of the window.

To set the Auto shrink option for a database using T-SQL code:

1. Click **Start**, point to **Programs**, point to **Microsoft SQL Server**, and then click **Query Analyzer**. The Connect to SQL Server dialog box opens.

2. Verify that **(local)** is listed in the SQL Server text box, and that the **Windows authentication** radio button is selected, and then click **OK**. The SQL Query Analyzer window appears.

3. In the query window, type the following text:

   Alter database Company3
   set auto_shrink ON

   and then execute the query by pressing **F5**. A message appears in the bottom section of the query window indicating that the command completed successfully.

To rename a database and observe the resulting changes:

1. In the query window, delete the previous text, and then type the following text:

   exec sp_renamedb 'Company3', 'CompanyTHREE'

   Execute the query by pressing **F5**. A message appears in the bottom section of the query window indicating that the database name has been set.

2. To return to Windows Explorer, click the **Data** button on your taskbar. The contents of the data folder are displayed on the right. Notice the data and log files for the CompanyTHREE database are still named Company3DATA and Company3LOG.

3. To minimize Windows Explorer, click the **Minimize** button in the top-right corner of the window.

4. To minimize Query Analyzer, click the **Minimize** button in the top-right corner of the window. You are returned to Enterprise Manager.

To delete a database using Enterprise Manager:

1. Right-click the **CompanyTWO** database, and then click **Delete**. The Delete Database dialog box opens, as shown in Figure 5-8.

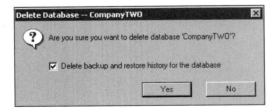

Figure 5-8 The Delete Database dialog box

2. Click **Yes**.

3. To close Enterprise Manager, click the **Close** button in the top-right corner of the window.

4. To return to Windows Explorer, click the **Data** button on your taskbar.

5. Notice that the CompanyTWO data and log files, and the Co_TWO_NFG_Data.NDF file have been deleted from the Data folder.

Lab 5.4 Changing Database Options; Renaming and Deleting Databases

To delete a database using the T-SQL command DROP DATABASE:

1. To return to Query Analyzer, click the **SQL Query Analyzer** button on your taskbar.

2. In the query window, delete the previous text, and then type the following text:

   drop database CompanyTHREE

   Execute the query by pressing **F5**. Two messages appear in the bottom section of the query window indicating that the data and log files were deleted.

3. To close Query Analyzer, click the **Close** button in the top-right corner of the window. The SQL Query Analyzer dialog box opens, asking if you want to save changes.

4. Click **No To All**. You are returned to Windows Explorer.

5. Notice that the CompanyTHREE data and log files have been deleted from the Data folder.

6. To close Windows Explorer, click the **Close** button in the top-right corner of the window.

Certification Objectives

Objectives for Microsoft Exam #70-228: Installing, Configuring, and Administering Microsoft SQL Server 2000 Enterprise Edition:

➤ Create and alter databases

➤ Add filegroups, configure filegroup usage

➤ Set database options by using the ALTER DATABASE or CREATE DATABASE statements

Review Questions

1. On what tab in the *database_name* Properties dialog box will you find the Use quoted identifiers option?
   a. General
   b. Filegroups
   c. Options
   d. Identifiers

2. Which of the following is false?
   a. A filegroup can be used by more than one database.
   b. A file can be a member of only one filegroup.
   c. Data and transaction log information cannot be part of the same filegroup.
   d. Transaction log files are never part of any filegroups.

3. What tool can be used to rename a database?
   a. Enterprise Manager
   b. Query Analyzer executing the ALTER DATABASE command
   c. Query Analyzer executing the system stored procedure sp_renamedb
   d. All of the above

4. Renaming a database will also rename:
   a. the primary data file
   b. any secondary data files
   c. the Log file
   d. None of the above

5. Deleting a database will also delete:
   a. the primary data file
   b. any secondary data files
   c. the Log file
   d. All of the above

LAB 5.5 CREATING TABLES IN A DATABASE

Objectives

The goal of this lab is to create two tables in the CompanyONE database.

Materials Required

This lab will require the following:

- Access to a computer running Windows 2000 Server, Windows 2000 Advanced Server, or Windows 2000 Datacenter Server with SQL Server 2000 installed
- The CompanyONE database (created in Lab 5.2)

Estimated completion time: **15 minutes**

Activity Background

Now that you created a new database and data and transaction logs, and configured the database, it is time to create the tables. Usually this task is left to the database designers. However, understanding how tables are created and their overall structure will make many other segments of your job as database administrator much easier. In this lab, you will create two tables for the CompanyONE database. The first table will hold company employee information, and the second will hold information about the different office locations.

Lab 5.5 Creating Tables in a Database 99

ACTIVITY

1. Boot your computer and log on, if necessary.

2. In Books Online, click the **Contents** tab. (See Lab 1.3 for instructions to start Books Online, if necessary.) Expand **Creating and Maintaining Databases**, expand **Tables**, and then double-click **Creating and Modifying a Table**. The "Creating and Modifying a Table" document appears in the Topic pane.

3. Read through the document, and click the link to read the Transact-SQL code used to create a table.

4. To close Books Online, click the **Close** button in the top-right corner of the window.

5. Click **Start**, point to **Programs**, point to **Microsoft SQL Server**, and then click **Enterprise Manager**. The SQL Server Enterprise Manager window appears.

6. Expand **Microsoft SQL Servers**, expand **SQL Server Group**, and then expand your *server_name*.

7. Expand **Databases**, and then expand the **CompanyONE** database.

8. Click **Tables**. The system-supplied tables are listed on the right of the window.

9. Right-click **Tables**, and then click **New Table**. The 2:New Table in 'CompanyONE' on '*server_name*' window appears.

This window is also known as the Table Designer.

10. Create the columns using the information in Table 5-1.

Table 5-1 Employee data for new table in CompanyONE

Column Name	Data Type	Length	Allow Nulls
LastName	varchar	50	No
FirstName	varchar	50	No
MiddleInit	char	1	Yes
SSN	numeric	9	No
Address1	char	50	No
Address2	char	50	Yes
City	varchar	20	No
State	char	2	No
Zip	numeric	9	No
Location	char	10	No

11. After you have created the 10 columns, click the SSN row by clicking the box to the left of the column name. Click the **Set primary key** button on the toolbar. The key icon appears to the left of the SSN row.

12. Click the **Save** button on the toolbar. The Choose Name dialog box opens. Type **C1Employee**, and then click **OK**.

13. To close the Table Designer window, click the lower of the two **Close** buttons in the top-right corner of the window.

14. Right-click **Tables**, and then click **New Table**. The 2:New Table in 'CompanyONE' on '*server_name*' window appears.

15. Create the columns using the information in Table 5-2.

Table 5-2 Office location data for new table in CompanyONE

Column Name	Data Type	Length	Allow Nulls
Location	char	10	No
OfficeAddress1	char	50	No
OfficeAddress2	char	50	Yes
OfficeCity	varchar	20	No
OfficeState	char	2	No
OfficeZip	numeric	9	No

16. After you have created the six columns, click the Location row by clicking the box to the left of the column name. Click the **Set primary key** button on the toolbar. The key icon appears to the left of the Location row.

17. Click the **Save** button on the toolbar. The Choose Name dialog box opens. Type **C1OfficeLocation**, and then click **OK**.

18. To close the Table Designer window, click the lower of the two **Close** buttons in the top-right corner of the window.

19. To close Enterprise Manager, click the **Close** button in the top-right corner of the window.

Review Questions

1. How many columns can be defined per table?
   a. 10
   b. 256
   c. 512
   d. 1024

2. Column names must be unique within a:
   a. table
   b. database
   c. filegroup
   d. server

3. In a T-SQL CREATE DATABASE statement, when can a column name be omitted?
   a. When the column is an identity column
   b. When the data type is timestamp
   c. When the column is a computed column
   d. When the column is an expression

4. Where are temporary tables stored?
   a. In the primary filegroup
   b. In the primary file
   c. In the secondary file
   d. In tempdb

5. How many characters can a table name be?
   a. 32
   b. 64
   c. 128
   d. 256

LAB 5.6 CREATING A FOREIGN KEY RELATIONSHIP

Objectives

The goal of this lab is to link the two tables created in Lab 5.5 with a foreign key relationship.

Materials Required

This lab will require the following:

➤ Access to a computer running Windows 2000 Server, Windows 2000 Advanced Server, or Windows 2000 Datacenter Server with SQL Server 2000 installed

➤ The CompanyONE database (created in Lab 5.2 and 5.5)

Chapter 5 Creating SQL Server 2000 Databases

Estimated completion time: **15 minutes**

Activity Background

Relational databases are complex entities, more than simple tables of rows and columns. In this lab, you will continue to build the CompanyONE database by adding a foreign key relationship between the two tables created in Lab 5.5. Remember, when you create a foreign key in Enterprise Manager, you can start with either table. But, the primary key table must have the linking column as it's primary key. Once the relationship is created, you will create a diagram of the database to illustrate the relationship.

Activity

1. Boot your computer and log on, if necessary.

2. Click **Start**, point to **Programs**, point to **Microsoft SQL Server**, and then click **Enterprise Manager**. The SQL Server Enterprise Manager window appears.

3. Expand **Microsoft SQL Servers**, expand **SQL Server Group**, and then expand your *server_name*.

4. Expand **Databases**, and then expand the **CompanyONE** database.

5. Click **Tables**. The user and system-supplied tables are listed on the right of the window.

6. Right-click the **C1OfficeLocation table**, and then click **Design Table**. The 2: Design Table 'C1OfficeLocation' in 'CompanyONE' on '*server_name*' window appears.

7. Click the **Table and Index Properties** button on the toolbar. The Properties dialog box opens. Click the **Relationships** tab.

8. Click the **New** button to create a new relationship. SQL Server automatically fills in the Selected relationship and Relationship name.

9. Click the Primary key table list arrow, and then click **C1OfficeLocation**. Click the list arrow in the field box, and choose **Location**, as shown in Figure 5-9.

Lab 5.6 Creating a Foreign Key Relationship 103

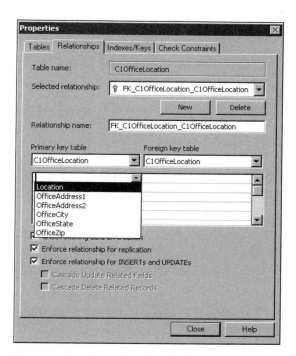

Figure 5-9 Choosing the field in the Primary key table

10. Click the Foreign key table list arrow, and then click **C1Employee**. Notice how the text in the Selected relationship and Relationship name text boxes changes as you make these selections.

11. Click the list arrow in the field box, and choose **Location**, as shown in Figure 5-10.

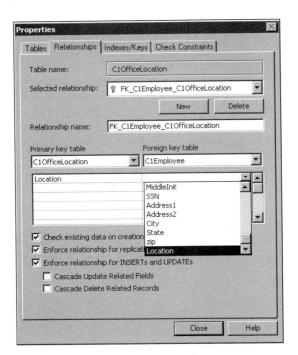

Figure 5-10 Choosing the field in the Foreign key table

12. Click **Close**. The Properties dialog box closes and the foreign key relationship has been created.

13. To close the Table Designer window, click the lower of the two **Close** buttons in the top-right corner of the window. The SQL Server Enterprise Manager dialog box opens, asking if you want to save changes to the table.

14. Click **Yes**. The Save dialog box opens indicating that changes will be saved to both the C1OfficeLocation and C1Employee tables. Click **Yes**.

15. Under CompanyONE, right-click **Diagrams**, and then click **New Database Diagram**. The Create Database Diagram Wizard opens.

16. Click **Next**.

17. Click **Add>** twice to add the C1Employee and the C1OfficeLocation tables to the diagram.

18. Click **Next**. Click **Finish**. The 2: New Diagram in 'CompanyONE' on '*server_name*' is displayed.

19. Place the mouse pointer over the bar connecting the two tables to display the foreign key relationship name, as shown in Figure 5-11.

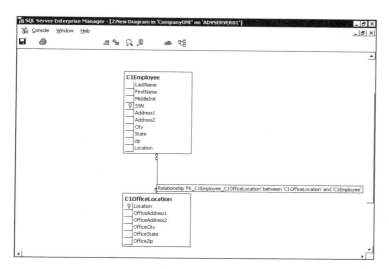

Figure 5-11 Displaying a foreign key relationship name in a database diagram

20. To close the New Diagram window, click the lower of the two **Close** buttons in the top-right corner of the window. The SQL Server Enterprise Manager dialog box opens, asking if you want to save changes to the diagram.

21. Click **Yes**. The Save As dialog box opens.

22. Click **OK** to accept the default name.

23. To close Enterprise Manager, click the **Close** button in the top-right corner of the window.

Review Questions

1. In Enterprise Manager, how can you view the relationships defined for a table?
   a. Right-click the table name, then click Properties.
   b. Double-click the table name.
   c. Click the Table and Index Properties button in Table Designer, and then click the Relationships tab.
   d. Click the Table and Index Properties button in Table Designer, and then click the Indexes/Keys tab.

2. If you are creating a foreign key relationship between two tables that already have data in them, how can you instruct SQL Server to check this existing data?
   a. Check the Check existing data on creation check box.
   b. Uncheck the Check existing data on creation check box.
   c. Check the Don't check existing data on creation check box.
   d. Uncheck the Don't check existing data on creation check box.

3. How can you instruct SQL Server to automatically update foreign key values of a relationship whenever the primary key value is updated?
    a. Check the Enforce relationship for replication check box.
    b. Check the Cascade Update Related Fields check box.
    c. Check the Cascade Delete Related Fields check box.
    d. Check the Update foreign key values check box.

4. After the creation of a foreign key relationship, it is saved as part of:
    a. the primary key table
    b. the foreign key table
    c. the database as a separate entity
    d. both the primary key and foreign key tables

5. In a database diagram, the graphic that represents the foreign key relationship is a:
    a. bar
    b. bar with a key icon on one end
    c. bar with an infinity icon on one end
    d. bar with a key icon on one end and an infinity icon on the other end

CHAPTER SIX

OPTIMIZING AND TROUBLESHOOTING DATABASES

Labs included in this chapter

- ➤ Lab 6.1 Recreating Indexes to Change the Fill Factor
- ➤ Lab 6.2 Using an Execution Plan to Create Statistics
- ➤ Lab 6.3 Recompiling Stored Procedures
- ➤ Lab 6.4 Using SQL Profiler to Monitor Stored Procedures

Microsoft MCSE Exam #70-228 Objectives	
Objective	Lab
Optimize database performance; considerations include indexing, locking, and recompiling.	6.1, 6.2, 6.3
Manage database fragmentation	6.1
Troubleshoot transactions and locking by using SQL Profiler, SQL Server Enterprise Manager, or Transact-SQL	6.4

LAB 6.1 RECREATING INDEXES TO CHANGE THE FILL FACTOR

Objectives

The goal of this lab is to re-create several indexes on a table in the Northwind database, and to view how a lower fill factor increases the size of an index (and therefore the database that contains that index).

Materials Required

This lab will require the following:

> ➤ Access to a computer running Windows 2000 Server, Windows 2000 Advanced Server, or Windows 2000 Datacenter Server with SQL Server 2000 installed

Estimated completion time: **30 minutes**

Activity Background

The fill factor option is used when creating indexes on tables, and indicates how much space should be left in the index pages for new and updated data. As a database administrator, you must consider this option when creating new indexes, to insure optimum database performance. If the index pages get full, and new data is inserted, then SQL Server must make room by executing a page split. Page splits take time and resources, and will slow down other transactions on the database. The fill factor option is only considered at the time of index creation and is not maintained. Therefore, you may need to delete (or drop) an existing index in order to re-create it with a new fill factor.

Activity

1. Boot your computer, and log on by pressing **Ctrl+Alt+Del**. In the Log On to Windows window, type your user name and password in the text boxes, and then press **Enter**. The Windows 2000 desktop appears on your screen.

2. Click **Start**, point to **Programs**, point to **Microsoft SQL Server**, and then click **Books Online**. The SQL Server Books Online window appears.

3. Click the **Contents** tab. Expand **Creating and Maintaining Databases**, expand **Indexes**, and then expand **Designing an Index**. Double-click **Fill Factor**. The "Fill Factor" document appears in the Topic pane.

4. Read through the document.

5. To close Books Online, click the **Close** button in the top-right corner of the window.

6. Click **Start**, point to **Programs**, point to **Microsoft SQL Server**, and then click **Enterprise Manager**. The SQL Server Enterprise Manager window appears.

7. Expand **Microsoft SQL Servers**, expand **SQL Server Group**, expand your *server_name*, and then expand **Databases**.

Lab 6.1 Recreating Indexes to Change the Fill Factor

8. Right-click the **Northwind** database, and then click **Properties**. The Northwind Properties dialog box opens.
9. Click the **General** tab, if necessary.
10. Write down the values listed for Size and Space available.
11. Click **Cancel**.
12. Click **Start**, point to **Programs**, point to **Microsoft SQL Server**, and then click **Query Analyzer**. The Connect to SQL Server dialog box opens.
13. Verify that **(local)** is listed in the SQL Server text box, and that the **Windows authentication** radio button is selected, and then click **OK**. The SQL Query Analyzer window appears.
14. If the Object Browser window is not visible, activate it by pressing **F8**.
15. In the Object Browser window, expand **Northwind**, expand **User Tables**, expand **dbo.Customers**, and then expand **Indexes**.
16. Right-click the **City** index, and then click **Edit**. The Edit Existing Index dialog box opens.
17. Click **Edit SQL**. The Edit Transact-SQL Script dialog box opens.
18. Read the T-SQL code, and then click **Cancel**.
19. Under Index options, click to place a check for **Fill factor**, and change the fill factor amount to **50**, as shown in Figure 6-1.

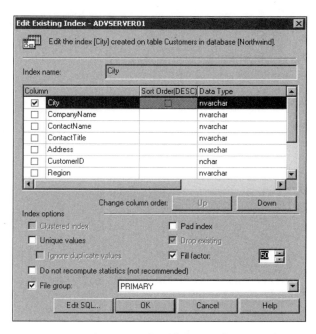

Figure 6-1 Changing the fill factor for an index

20. Click **Edit SQL**. The Edit Transact-SQL Script dialog box opens. Notice the change to the T-SQL code.

21. Click **Execute**. The Edit Transact-SQL Script dialog box opens, indicating that the script executed successfully.

22. Click **OK**. You are returned to Query Analyzer.

23. Repeat steps 16 and 19 through 22 to change the fill factor to 50 for the remaining three indexes (CompanyName, PostalCode, and Region).

24. To close Query Analyzer, click the **Close** button in the top-right corner of the window. You are returned to Enterprise Manager.

25. Right-click the **Northwind** database, and then click **Properties**. The Northwind Properties dialog box opens.

26. Click the **General** tab, if necessary.

27. Compare the values listed for Size and Space available with the original figures you wrote down at the beginning of this lab.

28. Click **Cancel**.

29. To close Enterprise Manager, click the **Close** button in the top-right corner of the window.

Certification Objectives

Objectives for Microsoft Exam #70-228: Installing, Configuring, and Administering Microsoft SQL Server 2000 Enterprise Edition:

➤ Optimize database performance; considerations include indexing, locking, and recompiling

➤ Manage database fragmentation

Review Questions

1. What percentage of data is moved to a new page when a new row is added to a full index page?
    a. 20
    b. 40
    c. 50
    d. 70

2. Which fill factor will ensure the least amount of disk storage needed (at the time of creation)?
    a. 10
    b. 50
    c. 80
    d. 100

3. Which fill factor will ensure the least amount of page splits needed?
   a. 10
   b. 50
   c. 80
   d. 100

4. What is the default fill factor (when none is specified)?
   a. 10
   b. 50
   c. 80
   d. 100

5. What system stored procedure is used to change the default fill factor for all new indexes created?
   a. sp_fillfactor
   b. sp_configure
   c. sp_changefillfactor
   d. sp_configurefillfactor

LAB 6.2 USING AN EXECUTION PLAN TO CREATE STATISTICS

Objectives

The goal of this lab is to create and update statistics on a table using an execution plan.

Materials Required

This lab will require the following:

> ➤ Access to a computer running Windows 2000 Server, Windows 2000 Advanced Server, or Windows 2000 Datacenter Server with SQL Server 2000 installed

Est mated completion time: 30 minutes

Activity Background

SQL Server 2000 creates and updates statistical information about your databases automatically, and uses this information to decide how to best execute a query. This information may, however, become out-of-date, and you as the database administrator may need to manually create and update these statistics. You can also change the amount of data that is sampled to create the statistics. In this lab, you will create an execution plan for a simple select query, and then use that plan to create and then update the statistics for a table.

ACTIVITY

1. Boot your computer and log on, if necessary.

2. Click **Start**, point to **Programs**, point to **Microsoft SQL Server**, and then click **Books Online**. The SQL Server Books Online window appears.

3. Click the **Contents** tab. Expand **Optimizing Database Performance**, expand **Query Tuning**, and then expand **Analyzing a Query**. Double-click **Graphically Displaying the Execution Plan Using SQL Query Analyzer**.

4. Read through the document displayed in the Topic pane.

5. To close Books Online, click the **Close** button in the top-right corner of the window.

6. Click **Start**, point to **Programs**, point to **Microsoft SQL Server**, and then click **Query Analyzer**. The Connect to SQL Server dialog box opens.

7. Verify that **(local)** is listed in the SQL Server text box, and that the **Windows authentication** radio button is selected, and then click **OK**. The SQL Query Analyzer window appears.

8. If the Object Browser window is not visible, activate it by pressing **F8**.

9. Click the **Query** menu, and then click **Show Execution Plan**.

10. In the Object Browser window, expand **Northwind**, expand **User Tables**, expand **dbo.Customers**, and then expand **Indexes**.

11. In the query window, type the following text:

    use Northwind
    select * from customers
    where city = 'london'
    go

    and execute the command by pressing **F5**. Six records are displayed in the Grids pane of the results section at the bottom of the query window.

12. Click the **Execution Plan** tab at the bottom of the query window.

13. Place your mouse pointer over each of the three icons in the execution plan, and read the information displayed.

The information displayed as the mouse is moved over each of the icons is called ToolTip information.

14. Right-click the **Index Seek (Customers.City)** icon, and then click **Manage Statistics**. The Manage Statistics dialog box opens.

15. Verify that **Northwind** is listed in the Database text box, and **dbo.Customers** is listed in the Table/view text box, and then click **New**. The Create Statistics dialog box opens.

16. In the Name text box, type **newcitystats**.

17. In the list of columns, click to place a check in the box to the left of **City**.

18. Under Amount of data to sample, click **Sample all the data**, as shown in Figure 6-2.

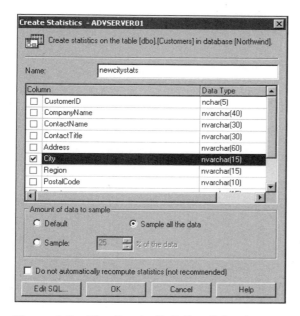

Figure 6-2 The Create Statistics dialog box

19. Click **Edit SQL**. The Edit Transact-SQL Script dialog box opens.

20. Read the Create Statistics statement, and then click **Execute**. The Edit Transact-SQL Script dialog box opens indicating that the script executed successfully.

21. Click **OK**. You are returned to the Manage Statistics dialog box with the newcitystats listed under Existing statistics.

22. Click **Update**. The Update Statistics dialog box opens.

23. Under Select statistics to update, click to place a check in the box to the left of **newcitystats**.

24. Under Amount of data to sample, click **Sample 25% of the data**, and then click **Edit SQL**.

25. Read the Update Statistics statement, and then click **Execute**. The Edit Transact-SQL Script dialog box opens indicating that the script executed successfully.

26. Click **OK**. You are returned to the Manage Statistics dialog box.
27. Click **Close**. You are returned to Query Analyzer.
28. To close Query Analyzer, click the **Close** button in the top-right corner of the window. The SQL Query Analyzer dialog box opens, asking if you want to save changes.
29. Click **No To All**.

Certification Objectives

Objectives for Microsoft Exam #70-228: Installing, Configuring, and Administering Microsoft SQL Server 2000 Enterprise Edition:

➤ Optimize database performance; considerations include indexing, locking, and recompiling

Review Questions

1. How is a graphical execution plan output read?
   a. Top to bottom
   b. Right to left
   c. Left to right
   d. Right to left and top to bottom

2. Looking at an execution plan output, how can you tell that the query optimizer has issued a warning?
   a. The physical operator is displayed in red
   b. The logical operator is displayed in red
   c. The physical operator is displayed with an X over it
   d. The logical operator is displayed with an X over it

3. Which piece of ToolTip information indicates the cost to the query optimizer in executing this operation, including the cost of this operation as a percentage of the total cost of the query?
   a. I/O cost
   b. CPU cost
   c. Cost
   d. Subtree cost

4. Which of the following T-SQL statements creates statistics named Stats1 on a column Col1 in a table Table1, sampling all the data in the table?
   a. CREATE STATISTICS Stats1 ON Table1 (Col1)
   b. CREATE STATISTICS Stats1 ON Table1 (Col1) SAMPLE ALL
   c. CREATE STATISTICS WITH FULLSCAN Stats1 ON Table1 (Col1)
   d. CREATE STATISTICS Stats1 ON Table1 (Col1) WITH FULLSCAN

5. Which of the following T-SQL statements updates statistics named Stats1 on a column Col1 in a table Table1, sampling 25% of the data in the table?
   a. UPDATE STATISTICS Table1 (Col1) Stats1 WITH SAMPLE 25 PERCENT
   b. UPDATE STATISTICS Table1 (Stats1) WITH SAMPLE 25 PERCENT
   c. UPDATE STATISTICS WITH SAMPLE 25 PERCENT Table1 (Col1) Stats1
   d. UPDATE STATISTICS WITH SAMPLE 25 PERCENT Table1 (Stats1)

LAB 6.3 RECOMPILING STORED PROCEDURES

Objectives

The goal of this lab is to recompile all the stored procedures that rely on a single table.

Materials Required

This lab will require the following:

➤ Access to a computer running Windows 2000 Server, Windows 2000 Advanced Server, or Windows 2000 Datacenter Server with SQL Server 2000 installed

Estimated completion time: **15 minutes**

Activity Background

SQL Server 2000 has a place in memory called a procedure cache, which it uses to store already compiled stored procedures (execution plans). These execution plans are stored to save the time of recompiling a stored procedure every time it is used. When certain changes are made to the underlying structure that a stored procedure relies on, it may need to be recompiled. Sometimes the SQL Server will recompile a stored procedure automatically, and other times recompilation may need to be done manually.

ACTIVITY

1. Boot your computer and log on, if necessary.

2. Click **Start**, point to **Programs**, point to **Microsoft SQL Server**, and then click **Books Online**. The SQL Server Books Online window appears.

3. Click the **Contents** tab. Expand **Creating and Maintaining Databases**, expand **Stored Procedures**, and then double-click **Recompiling a Stored Procedure**.

4. Read through the document displayed in the Topic pane.

5. Click the link near the bottom of the document to view the Transact-SQL code to recompile a stored procedure the next time it is run.

6. To close Books Online, click the **Close** button in the top-right corner of the window.

7. Click **Start**, point to **Programs**, point to **Microsoft SQL Server**, and then click **Query Analyzer**. The Connect to SQL Server dialog box opens.

8. Verify that **(local)** is listed in the SQL Server text box, and that the **Windows authentication** radio button is selected, and then click **OK**. The SQL Query Analyzer window appears.

9. If the Object Browser window is not visible, activate it by pressing **F8**.

10. In the Object Browser window, expand **Northwind**, and then expand **User Tables**.

11. Expand **dbo.Orders**, and then expand **Dependencies**. The stored procedures that rely on this table are listed.

12. In the query window, type the following text:
    use Northwind
    exec sp_recompile 'orders'
    go
    and execute the command by pressing **F5**. The message "Object 'orders' was successfully marked for recompilation." appears in the bottom section of the query window.

13. To close Query Analyzer, click the **Close** button in the top-right corner of the window. The SQL Query Analyzer dialog box opens, asking if you want to save changes.

14. Click **No To All**.

Certification Objectives

Objectives for Microsoft Exam #70-228: Installing, Configuring, and Administering Microsoft SQL Server 2000 Enterprise Edition:

➤ Optimize database performance; considerations include indexing, locking, and recompiling

Review Questions

1. When will the automatic recompilation of a stored procedure occur?
   a. Every time the stored procedure is run
   b. If an underlying table used by the stored procedure is changed
   c. A new index is added to a table used by the stored procedure
   d. Never

2. You want to recompile a stored procedure. You execute the sp_recompile system stored procedure for that stored procedure. When will the recompilation happen?
   a. Immediately
   b. The next time the stored procedure is displayed
   c. The next time the stored procedure is run
   d. The next time the SQL server is restarted

3. How can you specify that a stored procedure's execution plan not be kept in the procedure cache, and instead have the stored procedure recompiled every time it is run?
   a. Create the stored procedure with the WITH RECOMPILE option in its definition
   b. Create the stored procedure with the NO PROCEDURE CACHE option in its definition
   c. Execute the sp_configure system stored procedure, and set the recompile option to YES
   d. Execute the sp_configure system stored procedure, and set the procedure cache option to NO

4. Which of the following T-SQL statements will recompile the Proc1 stored procedure, which depends on the Table1 table the next time it is run?
   a. sp_recompile Table1, Proc1
   b. sp_recompile Table1, Proc1 NEXT
   c. sp_recompile 'Proc1'
   d. sp_recompile 'Proc1' NEXT

5. Which of the following T-SQL statements will recompile all of the stored procedures that depend on the Table1 table the next time it is run?
   a. sp_recompile Table1 NEXT
   b. sp_recompile Table1
   c. sp_recompile 'Table1' NEXT
   d. sp_recompile 'Table1'

LAB 6.4 USING SQL PROFILER TO MONITOR STORED PROCEDURES

Objectives

The goal of this lab is to become familiar with the SQL Profiler tool.

Materials Required

This lab will require the following:

> ➤ Access to a computer running Windows 2000 Server, Windows 2000 Advanced Server, or Windows 2000 Datacenter Server with SQL Server 2000 installed

Estimated completion time: 25 minutes

Activity Background

SQL Profiler is a monitoring tool used to monitor many different activities for many different reasons. You may be troubleshooting a slow running query, or perhaps tracking normal activity for a benchmark. Whatever the reason, SQL Profiler can gather a large amount of information. You can simply display this information, or save it either to a file or a table, where it can be reviewed or replayed. One word of caution—be careful what you monitor. These files can become very large very quickly!

Activity

1. Boot your computer and log on, if necessary.

2. Click **Start**, point to **Programs**, point to **Microsoft SQL Server**, and then click **Books Online**. The SQL Server Books Online window appears.

3. In the Navigation pane, click the **Search** tab. Type the text **"SQL Profiler"** (including the quotes) into the search criteria text box, and then click **List Topics**. The results of the search are displayed.

4. Under Select topic, double-click **Monitoring with SQL Profiler**.

5. Read through the document displayed in the Topic pane.

6. To close Books Online, click the **Close** button in the top-right corner of the window.

7. Click **Start**, point to **Programs**, point to **Microsoft SQL Server**, and then click **Profiler**. The SQL Profiler window appears.

8. Click the **File** menu, point to **New**, and then click **Trace**. The Connect to SQL Server dialog box opens.

9. Verify that **(local)** is listed in the SQL Server text box, and that the **Windows authentication** radio button is selected, and then click **OK**. The Trace Properties dialog box opens.

10. On the General tab, in the Trace name text box, type **NewSPTrace**.

11. Click the **Template name** list arrow, and then click the **SQLProfilerSP_Counts** template.

12. Click **Save to file**. The Save As dialog box opens.

13. Click the **Save in** list arrow, and then click the drive letter on which SQL Server is installed.

14. Click **Save**. You are returned to the Trace Properties dialog box.

15. Click the **Events** tab. Notice that only one event, stored procedure starting, is going to be monitored.

Lab 6.4 Using SQL Profiler to Monitor Stored Procedures

16. Under Available event classes, expand **Stored Procedures**.
17. Click **SP:StmtStarting**, and then click **Add**.
18. Repeat Step 17 to add **SP:StmtCompleted**.
19. Click **Run**. The NewSPTrace dialog box opens.
20. Click **Start**, point to **Programs**, point to **Microsoft SQL Server**, and then click **Query Analyzer**. The Connect to SQL Server dialog box opens.
21. Verify that **(local)** is listed in the SQL Server text box, and that the **Windows authentication** radio button is selected, and then click **OK**. The SQL Query Analyzer window appears.
22. If the Object Browser window is not visible, activate it by pressing **F8**.
23. In the Object Browser window, expand **Northwind**, and then expand **Stored Procedures**.
24. Right-click the **dbo.CustOrderHist** stored procedure, and then click **Open**. The Execute Procedure dialog box opens.
25. In the Value text box, type **AROUT**, as shown in Figure 6-3.

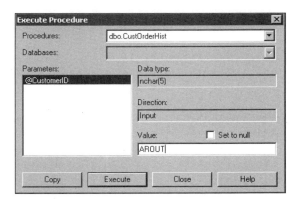

Figure 6-3 The Execute Procedure dialog box

26. Click **Execute**. The text of the stored procedure appears in the top of the query window, and the results are displayed in the bottom.
27. Repeat steps 22, 23, and 24 twice, using **CHOPS** and **GREAL** for the customerID value.
28. To close Query Analyzer, click the **Close** button in the top-right corner of the window. The SQL Query Analyzer dialog box opens, asking if you want to save changes.
29. Click **No To All**. You are returned to SQL Profiler.
30. Click the **File** menu, and then click **Stop Trace**.

31. Scroll to the top of the results and notice the three entries for the three times the stored procedure was run, each having the same Database ID (6), but different SPIDs.
32. To close SQL Profiler, click the **Close** button in the top-right corner of the window.

Certification Objectives

Objectives for Microsoft Exam #70-228: Installing, Configuring, and Administering Microsoft SQL Server 2000 Enterprise Edition:

➤ Troubleshoot transactions and locking by using SQL Profiler, SQL Server Enterprise Manager, or Transact-SQL

Review Questions

1. Using SQL Profiler, where can you save the output of a trace?
   a. In a file
   b. In a table
   c. In an Excel spreadsheet
   d. In a file or a table

2. Which event class is a collection of events that are produced when data and/or log files grow and/or shrink?
   a. Cursors
   b. Database
   c. Locks
   d. Security Audit

3. Which event class is a collection of event classes that are produced when database objects are created, opened, closed, dropped, or deleted?
   a. Objects
   b. Performance
   c. Scans
   d. Security Audit

4. Which event class is a collection of database audit event classes?
   a. Database
   b. Objects
   c. Server
   d. Security Audit

5. Which event class is a collection of server control and server memory change events?
   a. Memory
   b. Control
   c. Server
   d. TSQL

CHAPTER SEVEN

PERFORMING DISASTER RECOVERY OPERATIONS

Labs included in this chapter

- ➤ Lab 7.1 Setting the Recovery Model for Databases
- ➤ Lab 7.2 Creating Backup Devices
- ➤ Lab 7.3 Performing Windows 2000 and Database Backups
- ➤ Lab 7.4 Recovering the System State and Restoring Databases
- ➤ Lab 7.5 Performing Integrity Checks on a Database Using DBCC Commands
- ➤ Lab 7.6 Creating a Database Maintenance Plan

Microsoft MCSE Exam #70-228 Objectives	
Objective	Lab
Perform backups	7.3
Recover the system state and restore data	7.4
Perform integrity checks; methods include configuring the Database Maintenance Plan Wizard and using the Database Consistency Checker (DBCC)	7.5, 7.6

LAB 7.1 SETTING THE RECOVERY MODEL FOR DATABASES

Objectives

The goal of this lab is to change the recovery model for a database using both Enterprise Manager and Query Analyzer.

Materials Required

This lab will require the following:

➤ Access to a computer running Windows 2000 Server, Windows 2000 Advanced Server, or Windows 2000 Datacenter Server with SQL Server 2000 installed

Estimated completion time: **20 minutes**

Activity Background

The recovery model of a database is a very important setting. It defines how a database can be backed up, how much work may be lost, and whether the database can be recovered back to a specific point in time in the event of a failure. In this activity, you will change the recovery model using Enterprise Manager and T-SQL code in Query Analyzer.

ACTIVITY

1. Boot your computer, and log on by pressing **Ctrl+Alt+Del**. In the Log On to Windows window, type your user name and password in the text boxes, and then press **Enter**. The Windows 2000 desktop appears on your screen.

2. Click **Start**, point to **Programs**, point to **Microsoft SQL Server**, and then click **Books Online**. The SQL Server Books Online window appears.

3. In the Navigation pane, click the **Search** tab. Type **recovery model** in the search criteria text box, and then click **List Topics**. The results of the search are displayed.

4. Under Select topic, double-click **Selecting a Recovery Model**. Read through the information displayed.

5. To close Books Online, click the **Close** button in the top-right corner of the window.

6. Click **Start**, point to **Programs**, point to **Microsoft SQL Server**, and then click **Enterprise Manager**. The SQL Server Enterprise Manager window appears.

7. Expand **Microsoft SQL Servers**, expand **SQL Server Group**, expand your *server_name*, and then expand **Databases**.

Lab 7.1 Setting the Recovery Model for Databases 123

8. Right-click the **Northwind** database, and then click **Properties**. The Northwind Properties dialog box opens.

9. Click the **Options** tab.

10. Click the Model list arrow, and choose **Full**, as shown in Figure 7-1.

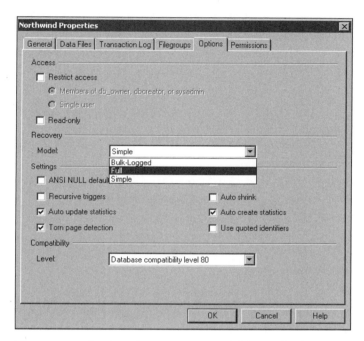

Figure 7-1 Setting the recovery model for a database using Enterprise Manager

11. Click **OK**.

12. Repeat steps 8 through 11 to set the recovery model for the pubs database to Bulk-Logged.

13. Click the **Tools** menu, and then click **SQL Query Analyzer**. The SQL Query Analyzer window appears.

14. Verify that pubs is listed in the Database list.

The database you have open while using Enterprise Manager will remain the current database when you launch Query Analyzer.

15. In the query window, type the following text:

    alter database pubs
    set recovery simple
    go

    and execute the command by pressing **F5**. The message "The command(s) completed successfully" is displayed in the Messages tab.

16. To close Query Analyzer, click the **Close** button in the top-right corner of the window. The SQL Query Analyzer dialog box opens, asking if you want to save changes.

17. Click **No To All**. You are returned to Enterprise Manager.

18. Right-click the **pubs** database, and then click **Properties**. The pubs Properties dialog box opens.

19. Click the **Options** tab and verify that the recovery model is now set to Simple.

20. Click **Cancel**.

21. To close Enterprise Manager, click the **Close** button in the top-right corner of the window.

Review Questions

1. Which recovery model can recover to any point in time?
   a. Full
   b. Simple
   c. Bulk-Logged
   d. All of the above

2. What is the default recovery model for a new database?
   a. Full
   b. Simple
   c. Bulk-Logged
   d. The recovery model for the model database

3. Transaction log backups are not used in which recovery model?
   a. Full
   b. Simple
   c. Bulk-Logged
   d. All of the above

4. On which tab of the Properties dialog box for a database can you set the recovery model?
   a. General
   b. Recovery
   c. Data Files
   d. Options

5. Which of the following is the correct syntax for the T-SQL statement to change the recovery model for a database named test from simple to full?
   a. ALTER DATABASE test
      SET RECOVERY MODEL full
   b. ALTER DATABASE test
      SET RECOVERY full
   c. ALTER DATABASE test
      CHANGE RECOVERY MODEL full
   d. ALTER DATABASE test
      CHANGE RECOVERY full

LAB 7.2 CREATING BACKUP DEVICES

Objectives

The goal of this lab is to create backup devices using both Enterprise Manager and Query Analyzer.

Materials Required

This lab will require the following:

> ➤ Access to a computer running Windows 2000 Server, Windows 2000 Advanced Server, or Windows 2000 Datacenter Server with SQL Server 2000 installed

Estimated completion time: **20 minutes**

Activity Background

Backup devices are nothing more than files used to store backups. No matter how you refer to them (either with the logical name you define or with the physical name of the actual file), they are still backup devices. In this activity, you will prepare to backup the Northwind database by creating two backup devices ahead of time. Another option is to create any needed backup devices as you are launching the backup. (You will do this in Lab 7.3).

ACTIVITY

1. Boot your computer and log on, if necessary.

2. Click **Start**, point to **Programs**, point to **Microsoft SQL Server**, and then click **Books Online**. The SQL Server Books Online window appears.

3. In the Navigation pane, click the **Search** tab. Type **"backup devices"** (including the quotation marks) in the search criteria text box, and then click **List Topics**. The results of the search are displayed.

4. Under Select topic, double-click **Backup Devices** in the Administering SQL Server location. (You may need to scroll down to locate this document.) Read through the information displayed.

5. At the bottom of this document, click the link to view the T-SQL code used to create a logical disk backup device.

6. To close Books Online, click the **Close** button in the top-right corner of the window.

7. Click **Start**, point to **Programs**, point to **Microsoft SQL Server**, and then click **Enterprise Manager**. The SQL Server Enterprise Manager window appears.

8. Expand **Microsoft SQL Servers**, expand **SQL Server Group**, and then expand your *server_name*.

9. Expand **Management**, right-click **Backup**, and then click **New Backup Device**. The Backup Device Properties dialog box opens.

10. In the Name text box, type **NWDataDevice**, as shown in Figure 7-2, and then click **OK**.

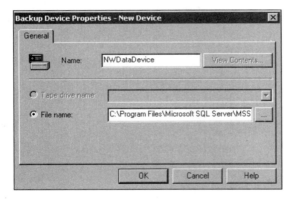

Figure 7-2 Creating a backup device using Enterprise Manager

11. Click the **Tools** menu, and then click **SQL Query Analyzer**. The SQL Query Analyzer window appears.

12. In the query window, type the following text:
    use master
    exec sp_addumpdevice 'disk',
    'NWLogDevice',
    'C:\program files\Microsoft SQL
        Server\mssql\backup\NWLogDevice.bak'
    go

    and execute the command by pressing **F5**. The message "(1 row(s) affected) 'Disk' device added." is displayed in the Messages tab, as shown in Figure 7-3.

Lab 7.2 Creating Backup Devices 127

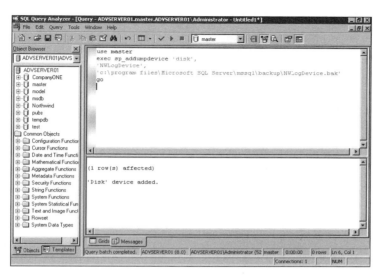

Figure 7-3 Creating a backup device using T-SQL

13. To close Query Analyzer, click the **Close** button in the top-right corner of the window. The SQL Query Analyzer dialog box opens, asking if you want to save changes.

14. Click **No To All**. You are returned to Enterprise Manager.

15. Click the **Action** menu, and then click **Refresh**. The NWLogDevice created using Query Analyzer is displayed.

16. To close Enterprise Manager, click the **Close** button in the top-right corner of the window.

17. Click **Start**, point to **Programs**, point to **Accessories**, and then click **Windows Explorer**. The My Documents window appears.

18. Expand **My Computer**, and then expand the drive on which SQL Server is installed.

19. Expand **Program Files**, expand **Microsoft SQL Server**, and then expand **MSSQL**.

20. Click to open the **BACKUP** folder. The contents of the data folder are displayed on the right. Notice that the two devices created previously are not listed.

Backup devices are not written to disk until they contain an actual backup file.

21. To close Windows Explorer, click the **Close** button in the top-right corner of the window.

Review Questions

1. Disk backup devices can be defined on a _____.
   a. local disk on a server
   b. remote disk on a shared network resource
   c. tape
   d. Both a and b.

2. Which type of device name can you use when backing up and restoring a database?
   a. The logical name only
   b. The physical name only
   c. The logical or physical backup device name interchangeably
   d. The operating system filename only

3. In the sp_addumpdevice syntax, which of the following is not a valid device type?
   a. Backup
   b. Disk
   c. Pipe
   d. Tape

4. Which of the following does not apply to the physical name argument of the sp_addumpdevice system stored procedure?
   a. It must include a full path.
   b. It can be NULL.
   c. It must follow the rules for operating system filenames or UNCs for network devices.
   d. It does not have a default value.

5. The stored procedure sp_addumpdevice adds a backup device to which table in the master database?
   a. sysdevices
   b. sysdumpdevices
   c. sysbackupdevices
   d. sysdiskdevices

LAB 7.3 PERFORMING WINDOWS 2000 AND DATABASE BACKUPS

Objectives

The goals of this lab are to back up the Windows 2000 system state data, and then back up the Northwind and pubs databases.

Lab 7.3 Performing Windows 2000 and Database Backups

Materials Required

This lab will require the following:

➤ Access to a computer running Windows 2000 Server, Windows 2000 Advanced Server, or Windows 2000 Datacenter Server with SQL Server 2000 installed

➤ The NWDataDevice and NWLogDevice backup devices

➤ Hard drive space to store the backup files

Estimated completion time: 30 minutes

Activity Background

Performing database backups is a big part of any database administrator's job. In Chapter 10 of this book, you will learn how to automate routine backups with the SQL server Agent. First, however, you must be thoroughly familiar with the different types of backups, and the many options that can be set for any given backup. Also, SQL server database backups must be coordinated with Windows 2000 backups so that if an entire server must be replaced, all the information needed is available. In this activity, you will first back up the system state data for your Windows 2000 server installation. This data includes the Windows 2000 Registry, files required to boot the computer, and other information. Next, you will back up the Northwind and pubs databases using Enterprise Manager and T-SQL code in Query Analyzer.

ACTIVITY

To back up the system state data of your Windows 2000 Server installation:

1. Boot your computer and log on, if necessary.
2. Click **Start**, point to **Programs**, point to **Accessories**, point to **System Tools**, and then click **Backup**. The Backup window appears.
3. Click **Backup Wizard**. The Backup Wizard starts.
4. Click **Next**. The What to Back Up screen appears.
5. Click the **Only back up the System State data** radio button, as shown in Figure 7-4, and then click **Next**. The Where to Store the Backup dialog box opens.

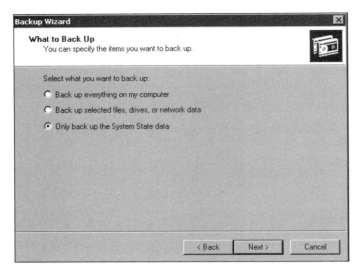

Figure 7-4 Selecting the system state data backup option in Backup Wizard

6. In the Backup media or file name text box, type **c:\ssdbackup.bkf**, and then click **Next**. The Completing the Backup Wizard screen appears.

7. Click **Finish**. The Selection Information and Backup Progress dialog boxes open and display information as the backup is performed.

8. Click **Close**. You are returned to the Backup window.

9. To close the Backup window, click the **Close** button in the top-right corner of the window.

To perform a full and differential backup of the Northwind database to the backup devices created in Lab 7.2, using Enterprise Manager:

1. Click **Start**, point to **Programs**, point to **Microsoft SQL Server**, and then click **Books Online**. The SQL Server Books Online window appears.

2. Click the **Search** tab. Type **backup/restore** in the search criteria text box, and then click **List Topics**. The results of the search are displayed.

3. Under Select topic, double-click **Backup/Restore Architecture** (in the SQL Server Architecture location). Read through the information displayed.

4. To close Books Online, click the **Close** button in the top-right corner of the window.

5. Click **Start**, point to **Programs**, point to **Microsoft SQL Server**, and then click **Enterprise Manager**. The SQL Server Enterprise Manager window appears.

6. Expand **Microsoft SQL Servers**, expand **SQL Server Group**, expand your *server_name*, and then expand **Databases**.

Lab 7.3 Performing Windows 2000 and Database Backups 131

7. Right-click the **Northwind** database, point to **All Tasks**, and then click **Backup Database**. The SQL Server Backup - Northwind dialog box opens.
8. In the Name text box, type **Northwind full backup**.
9. Under Backup, verify that the **Database - complete** radio button is selected.
10. Under Destination, click **Add**. The Select Backup Destination dialog box opens.
11. Click **Backup device**. Drop the list, and select **NWDataDevice**.
12. Click **OK**. You are returned to the SQL Server Backup dialog box.
13. Under Overwrite, click **Overwrite existing media** as shown in Figure 7-5.

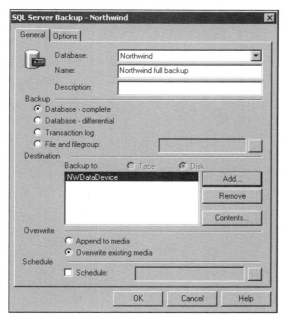

Figure 7-5 The SQL Server Backup - Northwind dialog box

14. Click **OK**. The Backup in Progress and SQL Server Enterprise Manager dialog boxes open as the backup is performed and completed.
15. Click **OK**. You are returned to the SQL Server Enterprise Manager window.
16. Right-click the **Northwind** database, point to **All Tasks**, and then click **Backup Database**. The SQL Server Backup dialog box opens.
17. In the Name text box, type **Northwind differential backup**.
18. Under Backup, click **Database - differential**.
19. Under Destination, verify that **NWDataDevice** is listed.
20. Under Overwrite, verify that **Append to media** is selected.

21. Click **OK**. The Backup in Progress and SQL Server Enterprise Manager dialog boxes open as the backup is performed and completed.
22. Click **OK**. You are returned to the SQL Server Enterprise Manager window.

To create a backup device and perform a full backup of the pubs database using Enterprise Manager:

1. Right-click the **pubs** database, point to **All Tasks**, and then click **Backup Database**. The SQL Server Backup dialog box opens.
2. In the Name text box, type **pubs full backup**.
3. Under Backup, verify that the **Database – complete** radio button is selected.

The Transaction Log and File and Filegroup options are not available in this screen because the pubs database is set to a Simple backup model.

4. Under Destination, click **Add**. The Select Backup Destination dialog box opens.
5. Click **Backup device**. In the Backup device list, click **<New Backup Device>** as shown in Figure 7-6. The Backup Device Properties dialog box opens.

Figure 7-6 Creating a backup device within the backup routine

6. In the Name text box, type **PubsDataDevice**, and then click **OK**. You are returned to the Select Backup Destination dialog box.
7. Click **OK**. You are returned to the SQL Server Backup dialog box.
8. Under Overwrite, click **Overwrite existing media**.
9. Click **OK**. The Backup in Progress and SQL Server Enterprise Manager dialog boxes open as the backup is performed and completed.
10. Click **OK**. You are returned to the SQL Server Enterprise Manager window.
11. To close Enterprise Manager, click the **Close** button in the top-right corner of the window.

Lab 7.3 Performing Windows 2000 and Database Backups

To perform a differential backup of the pubs database and a transaction log backup of the Northwind database using Query Analyzer:

1. Click **Start**, point to **Programs**, point to **Microsoft SQL Server**, and then click **Query Analyzer**. The Connect to SQL Server dialog box opens.

2. Verify that **(local)** is listed in the SQL Server text box, and that the **Windows authentication** radio button is selected, and then click **OK**. The SQL Query Analyzer window appears.

3. In the query window, type the following text:
   ```
   backup database pubs
   to pubsdatadevice
   with differential
   go
   ```
   and then press **F5**. A message appears in the Messages tab indicating that the backup statement completed successfully.

4. In the query window, edit the previous text to read:
   ```
   backup log northwind
   to nwlogdevice
   go
   ```
   and then press **F5**. A message appears in the Messages tab indicating that the backup statement completed successfully.

The backups created in the last two steps are appended to the end of the backups created using Enterprise Manager because the NOINIT option is the default, and does not have to be specified.

5. To close Query Analyzer, click the **Close** button in the top-right corner of the window. The SQL Query Analyzer dialog box opens, asking if you want to save changes.

6. Click **No To All**.

Certification Objectives

Objectives for Microsoft Exam #70-228: Installing, Configuring, and Administering Microsoft SQL Server 2000 Enterprise Edition:

➤ Perform backups

Review Questions

1. What type of backup copies only the database pages modified after the last full database backup?
   a. Full
   b. Transaction log
   c. Differential
   d. File or filegroup

2. Which of the following is not true of SQL Server backup and restore capabilities?
   a. Interrupted backup and restore operations must be completely redone.
   b. Backups can be performed while a database is in use.
   c. Databases can be automatically re-created during the restore process, if necessary.
   d. A set of backup history tables are maintained in the msdb database.

3. Which of the following is the correct syntax to perform a differential backup of a database named test to a backup device named testbackup?
   a. Backup test to testbackup with differential
   b. Backup database test to testbackup with differential
   c. Backup differential test to testbackup
   d. Differential backup database test to testbackup

4. Which of the following is the correct syntax to perform a transaction log backup of a database named test to a backup device named testbackup?
   a. Backup database test to testbackup with log
   b. Backup test to testbackup with log
   c. Backup log test to testbackup
   d. Log backup test to testbackup

5. Which of the following is the correct syntax to overwrite a full backup of a database named test onto a backup device named testbackup?
   a. Backup test to testbackup noinit
   b. Backup database test to testbackup with noinit
   c. Backup test to testbackup init
   d. Backup database test to testbackup with init

LAB 7.4 RECOVERING THE SYSTEM STATE AND RESTORING DATABASES

Objectives

The goals of this lab are to restore the Windows 2000 system state data, and then restore the Northwind and pubs databases.

Materials Required

This lab will require the following:

> Access to a computer running Windows 2000 Server, Windows 2000 Advanced Server, or Windows 2000 Datacenter Server with SQL Server 2000 installed

> The full and differential backups of the Northwind database stored in the NWDataDevice backup device

> The transaction log backup of the Northwind database stored in the NWLogDevice backup device

> The full and differential backups of the pubs database stored in the pubsdatadevice backup device

Estimated completion time: **25 minutes**

Activity Background

Restores are something that every database administrator dreads! But, similar to learning CPR, you must learn the restore process while hoping you will never have to use your knowledge. If your backups have been done properly, been kept up to date, and verified to ensure that the media is intact, the restore process should be relatively simple. As you will see, in most cases SQL Server will not allow backups to be applied in the wrong order. For example, neither Enterprise Manager nor the T-SQL code will recover a differential or transaction log backup until the full database has been restored.

ACTIVITY

To recover the system state data of your Windows 2000 Server installation:

1. Boot your computer and log on, if necessary.

2. Click **Start**, point to **Programs**, point to **Accessories**, point to **System Tools**, and then click **Backup**. The Backup window starts.

3. Click **Restore Wizard**. The Restore Wizard starts.

4. Click **Next**. The What to Restore screen appears.

5. Under What to restore, expand **File**, expand **Media created <date>**, and then expand **System State**. The Backup File Name dialog box opens.

6. Verify that **c:\ssdbackup.bkf** is listed in the Catalog backup file text box, and then click **OK**. The Operation Status appears briefly, and then you are returned to the What to Restore screen.

7. Click to place the blue check to the left of System State, and then click **Next**. The Completing the Restore Wizard screen appears.

8. Click **Finish**. The Enter Backup File Name dialog box opens.

9. Verify that **c:\ssdbackup.bkf** is listed in the Catalog backup file text box, and then click **OK**. The Restore Progress dialog box opens and displays information as the restore is performed.

10. Click **Close**. The Backup dialog box opens requesting that you shut down and restart your computer.

11. Click **Yes**. Your computer shuts down and restarts.

To restore the Northwind database using Enterprise Manager:

1. Log on to your computer by pressing **Ctrl+Alt+Del**. In the Log On to Windows window, type your user name and password in the text boxes, and then press **Enter**. The Windows 2000 desktop appears on your screen.

2. Click **Start**, point to **Programs**, point to **Microsoft SQL Server**, and then click **Enterprise Manager**. The SQL Server Enterprise Manager window appears.

3. Expand **Microsoft SQL Servers**, expand **SQL Server Group**, expand your *server_name*, and then expand **Databases**.

4. Right-click the **Northwind** database, point to **All Tasks**, and then click **Restore Database**. The Restore database dialog box opens, as shown in Figure 7-7.

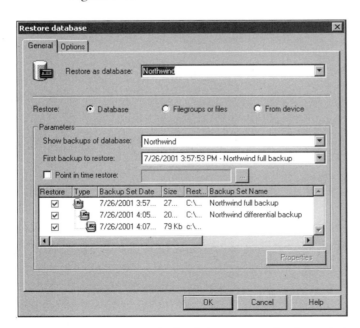

Figure 7-7 The General tab of the Restore database dialog box

Lab 7.4 Recovering the System State and Restoring Databases 137

5. Verify that all three backups are checked to be restored.

6. Click the **Options** tab. Under Recovery completion state, verify that **Leave database operational. No additional transaction logs can be restored.** is chosen.

7. Click **OK**. The Restore Progress and the SQL Server Enterprise Manager dialog boxes open indicating the progress and successful completion of the restore.

8. Click **OK**. You are returned to Enterprise Manager.

9. To close Enterprise Manager, click the **Close** button in the top-right corner of the window.

To restore the pubs database using Query Analyzer:

1. Click **Start**, point to **Programs**, point to **Microsoft SQL Server**, and then click **Query Analyzer**. The Connect to SQL Server dialog box opens.

2. Verify that **(local)** is listed in the SQL Server text box, and that the **Windows authentication** radio button is selected, and then click **OK**. The SQL Query Analyzer window appears.

3. In the query window, type the following text:
   **restore database pubs
   from pubsdatadevice
   with norecovery
   restore database pubs
   from pubsdatadevice
   with file = 2
   go**

   and then press **F5**. A message appears in the Messages tab indicating that both of the restore statements completed successfully.

The NORECOVERY option in the restore statement restores the full backup of the pubs database and leaves the database in a "nonoperational" state. This is done so that subsequent backups can be restored without the fear of users connecting to the database before all the restore process steps are completed.

The WITH FILE = 2 option in the RESTORE statement instructs the restore process to restore the second file on the media. This is done when multiple backups are saved to one backup device using the Append to media (or NOINIT) option.

4. To close Query Analyzer, click the **Close** button in the top-right corner of the window. The SQL Query Analyzer dialog box opens, asking if you want to save changes.

5. Click **No To All**.

Certification Objectives

Objectives for Microsoft Exam #70-228: Installing, Configuring, and Administering Microsoft SQL Server 2000 Enterprise Edition:

➤ Recover the sytem state and restore data

Review Questions

1. Which of the following is the correct syntax to perform a restore of a full backup of a database named test from a backup device named testbackup?
   a. RESTORE test from testbackup
   b. RESTORE database test from device testbackup
   c. RESTORE test from device testbackup
   d. RESTORE database test from testbackup

2. When restoring a full backup and several transaction log backups to a live database individually using Enterprise Manager, which option should be chosen on all but the last transaction log?
   a. Leave database operational. No additional transaction logs can be restored.
   b. Leave database nonoperational but able to restore additional transaction logs.
   c. Leave database read-only and able to restore additional transaction logs.
   d. WITH RECOVERY

3. When restoring a full backup and several transaction log backups as a set to a live database using Enterprise Manager, which option should be chosen?
   a. Leave database operational. No additional transaction logs can be restored.
   b. Leave database nonoperational but able to restore additional transaction logs.
   c. Leave database read-only and able to restore additional transaction logs.
   d. WITH NORECOVERY

4. When restoring a full backup and several transaction log backups to a live database using T-SQL statements, which option should be included on all but the last transaction log?
   a. WITH RECOVERY
   b. WITH NORECOVERY
   c. WITH STANDBY
   d. Leave database operational. No additional transaction logs can be restored.

5. When restoring a full backup and several transaction log backups to a live database using T-SQL statements, which option should be included on the last transaction log?
   a. WITH RECOVERY
   b. WITH NORECOVERY
   c. WITH STANDBY
   d. Leave database nonoperational but able to restore additional transaction logs.

Lab 7.5 Performing Integrity Checks on a Database Using DBCC Commands

Objectives

The goal of this lab is to perform integrity checks on the Northwind database using the DBCC commands CHECKDB and CHECKALLOC.

Materials Required

This lab will require the following:

➤ Access to a computer running Windows 2000 Server, Windows 2000 Advanced Server, or Windows 2000 Datacenter Server with SQL Server 2000 installed

Estimated completion time: **15 minutes**

Activity Background

DBCC commands have been included with many versions of SQL Server, but with each new release they have become less and less necessary. Unfortunately, even with SQL Server 2000's many advancements, problems can still occur. DBCC commands can be used simply to check an object, or correct problems that are found. In this lab, you will use both Books Online and the Help functionality built in to the commands to become familiar with a few commands and their syntax.

Activity

1. Boot your computer and log on, if necessary.

2. Click **Start**, point to **Programs**, point to **Microsoft SQL Server**, and then click **Books Online**. The SQL Server Books Online window appears.

3. Click the **Contents** tab. Expand **Transact-SQL Reference**. Scroll down to locate DBCC. Double-click **DBCC** to expand the list of commands in the Contents pane, and display the document "DBCC" in the topic pane.

4. Review the list of DBCC commands, and read through the information displayed.

5. To close Books Online, click the **Close** button in the top-right corner of the window.

6. Click **Start**, point to **Programs**, point to **Microsoft SQL Server**, and then click **Query Analyzer**. The Connect to SQL Server dialog box opens.

7. Verify that **(local)** is listed in the SQL Server text box, and that the **Windows authentication** radio button is selected, and then click **OK**. The SQL Query Analyzer window appears.

8. In the query window, type the following text:
   dbcc help ('?')
   and then press **F5**. The list of all DBCC commands for which help is available appears in the Messages tab.

9. In the query window, edit the previous text to read:
   dbcc help ('checkdb')
   and then press **F5**. The syntax of the command and a message indicating that the execution completed appear in the Messages tab.

10. In the query window, edit the previous text to read:
    dbcc help ('checkalloc')
    and then press **F5**. The syntax of the command and a message indicating that the execution completed appear in the Messages tab.

11. In the query window, edit the previous text to read:
    dbcc checkdb (northwind)
    and then press **F5**. Several messages appear in the Messages tab, ending with a message indicating the number of errors found and that the execution completed.

12. In the query window, edit the previous text to read:
    dbcc checkalloc (northwind)
    and then press **F5**. Several messages appear in the Messages tab, ending with a message indicating the number of errors found and that the execution completed.

13. To close Query Analyzer, click the **Close** button in the top-right corner of the window. The SQL Query Analyzer dialog box opens, asking if you want to save changes.

14. Click **No To All**.

Certification Objectives

Objectives for Microsoft Exam #70-228: Installing, Configuring, and Administering Microsoft SQL Server 2000 Enterprise Edition:

➤ Perform integrity checks; methods include configuring the Database Maintenance Plan Wizard and using the Database Consistency Checker (DBCC)

Review Questions

1. Which DBCC command will return syntax information for the specified DBCC statement?
   a. HELP
   b. SYNTAX
   c. STATEMENTHELP
   d. STATEMENTSYNTAX

2. Which DBCC command will check the allocation and structural integrity of all the objects in a specified database?
   a. CHECKDATABASE
   b. CHECKDB
   c. CHECKALLOCATION
   d. CHECKALLOC

3. Which DBCC command will check the consistency of disk space allocation structures for a specified database?
   a. CHECKDATABASE
   b. CHECKDB
   c. CHECKALLOCATION
   d. CHECKALLOC

4. Which DBCC command will rebuild one or more indexes for a table in a specified database?
   a. DBREINDEX
   b. DATABASEREINDEX
   c. DBREPAIR
   d. DATABASEREPAIR

5. Which DBCC command will display fragmentation information for the data and indexes of a specified table?
   a. CONTIG
   b. FRAG
   c. SHOWCONTIG
   d. SHOWFRAG

LAB 7.6 CREATING A DATABASE MAINTENANCE PLAN

Objectives

The goal of this lab is to create a database maintenance plan using Enterprise Manager.

Materials Required

This lab will require the following:

➤ Access to a computer running Windows 2000 Server, Windows 2000 Advanced Server, or Windows 2000 Datacenter Server with SQL Server 2000 installed

Chapter 7 Performing Disaster Recovery Operations

Estimated completion time: **20 minutes**

Activity Background

Now that you have learned how to back up and restore a database manually, let's see how to get SQL Server to do this work for you. The Database Maintenance Plan Wizard will walk you through the steps needed to create a complete yet manageable plan. Once a plan is in place, the SQL Server Agent carries out the steps using a schedule that you specify. The SQL Server Agent will be covered in more detail in Chapter 10.

ACTIVITY

1. Boot your computer and log on, if necessary.
2. Click **Start**, point to **Programs**, point to **Microsoft SQL Server**, and then click **Enterprise Manager**. The SQL Server Enterprise Manager window appears.
3. Expand **Microsoft SQL Servers**, expand **SQL Server Group**, and then expand your *server_name*.
4. Expand **Management**. Right-click **Database Maintenance Plans**, and then click **New Maintenance Plan**. The Database Maintenance Plan Wizard starts.
5. Click **Next**. The Select Databases screen appears.
6. Select **All databases**, and then click **Next**. The Update Data Optimization Information screen appears.
7. Click **Update statistics used by query optimizer**, and then click **Next**. The Database Integrity Check screen appears.
8. Click **Check database integrity**, then click **Exclude indexes**, as shown in Figure 7-8.

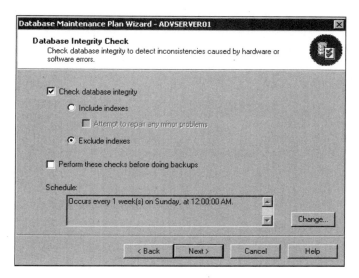

Figure 7-8 The Database Integrity Check screen in the Database Maintenance Plan Wizard

9. Click **Next**. The Specify the Database Backup Plan screen appears.

10. Verify that the **Back up the database as part of the maintenance plan** and the **Verify the integrity of the backup when complete** options are checked, and that the backup file location is **Disk**, and then click **Next**. The Specify Backup Disk Directory screen appears.

11. Under Directory in which to store the backup file, verify that **Use the default backup directory** is chosen, click **Create a subdirectory for each database**, and then click **Next**. The Specify the Transaction Log Backup Plan screen appears.

12. Click **Back up the transaction log as part of the maintenance plan**. Confirm that **Verify the integrity of the backup when complete** is checked, and that the backup file location is **Disk**, as shown in Figure 7-9

144   Chapter 7   Performing Disaster Recovery Operations

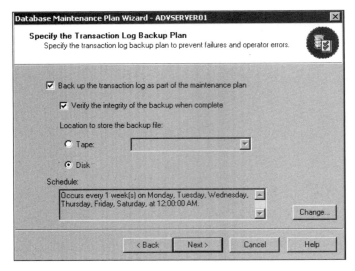

Figure 7-9 The Specify the Transaction Log Backup Plan screen in the Database Maintenance Plan Wizard

13. Click **Next**. The Specify Transaction Log Backup Disk Directory screen appears.

14. Under Directory in which to store the Backup file, verify that **Use the default backup directory** is chosen, click **Create a subdirectory for each database**, and then click **Next**. The Reports to Generate dialog box opens.

15. Click **Write report to text file in directory**, and then click the browse button (**...**). The Find Directory to Store Reports screen appears.

16. Notice the default directory, and then click **OK**.

17. Click **Next**. The Maintenance Plan History screen appears.

18. Under Local server, verify that **Write history to the msdb.dbo.sysdbmaintplan_history table on this server** and the **Limit rows in the table to** options are checked.

19. Click **Next**. The Completing the Database Maintenance Plan Wizard screen appears.

20. In the Plan name dialog box, type the name **AllDBMaintPlan**, and then click **Finish**. The SQL Server Enterprise Manager dialog box opens, asking you to ensure that the SQLServerAgent is running during the scheduled execution of this job. Click **OK**. You are returned to Enterprise Manager.

 The SQL Server Agent service allows an administrator to schedule routine tasks (Jobs) and send notification (Alerts) to individuals (Operators) regarding potential problems with a server.

21. Double-click the **AllDBMaintPlan** maintenance plan. The Database Maintenance Plan dialog box opens.
22. Review the information listed in the General, Optimizations, Integrity, Complete Backup, Transaction Log Backup and Reporting tabs. Click **Cancel**.
23. To close Enterprise Manager, click the **Close** button in the top-right corner of the window.

Certification Objectives

Objectives for Microsoft Exam #70-228: Installing, Configuring, and Administering Microsoft SQL Server 2000 Enterprise Edition:

➤ Perform integrity checks; methods include configuring the Database Maintenance Plan Wizard and using the Database Consistency Checker (DBCC)

Review Questions

1. Which of the following is not an optimization option in a Database Maintenance Plan?
   a. Reorganize data and index pages
   b. Recreate all indexes
   c. Update the statistics used by the query optimizer
   d. Remove unused space from the database files

2. Which of the following is not an integrity option in a Database Maintenance Plan?
   a. Check database integrity only
   b. Check database and index integrity
   c. Check index integrity only
   d. Check database integrity and attempt to repair any minor problems

3. Which of the following is not a backup option in a Database Maintenance Plan?
   a. Verify the integrity of the backup upon completion
   b. Back up to tape
   c. Remove files older than a specified amount of time
   d. Remove files larger than a specified amount of disk space

4. Which of the following is not a transaction log backup option in a Database Maintenance Plan?
   a. Back up the database
   b. Back up the transaction log
   c. Back up to disk
   d. Create a subdirectory for each database

5. Which of the following is not a reporting option in a Database Maintenance Plan?
   a. Write a text report to a text file
   b. Write the history to the msdb.dbo.sysdbmaintplan_history table
   c. Write the history to a table on a remote server
   d. Write a text report to the msdb.dbo.sysdbmaintplan_history table

CHAPTER EIGHT

SECURITY IN SQL SERVER 2000

Labs included in this chapter

- Lab 8.1 Creating SQL Server 2000 Logins
- Lab 8.2 Creating Database Users
- Lab 8.3 Creating User-Defined Database Roles
- Lab 8.4 Setting Statement and Object Permissions
- Lab 8.5 Testing Logins, Users, Roles, and Permissions

Microsoft MCSE Exam #70-228 Objectives	
Objective	Lab
Configure mixed security modes or Windows Authentication	8.1
Create and manage logins	8.1
Create and manage database users	8.2
Create and manage security roles; roles include application, database and server	8.3
Create roles to manage database security	8.3
Set permissions in a database; considerations include object permissions, object ownership, and statement permissions	8.4

LAB 8.1 CREATING SQL SERVER 2000 LOGINS

Objectives

The goal of this lab is to create SQL Server logins. Some of these logins will be tied directly to a Windows 2000 user or group account, and some will not.

Materials Required

This lab will require the following:

➤ Access to a computer running Windows 2000 Server, Windows 2000 Advanced Server, or Windows 2000 Datacenter Server with SQL Server 2000 installed

➤ The CompanyONE database, created in Lab 5.2

Estimated completion time: **60 minutes**

Activity Background

Securing your SQL server and the databases that reside on it is a major part of any database administrator's job. The first step in creating a secure environment is to create SQL Server logins. Armed with a valid SQL Server login, a user can gain access to the server only. Logins must then be mapped to database users to facilitate access to data in a database (which you will do in the next lab). In this lab, you will first change the authentication mode for your server from Windows Authentication mode to Mixed mode. This will allow you to create and test logins that are not tied to a Windows 2000 account. You will then execute a series of net commands to create the necessary Windows 2000 accounts. Finally, you will create the SQL Server logins using both Enterprise Manager and T-SQL commands.

ACTIVITY

To change the authentication mode for your SQL Server:

1. Boot your computer, and log on by pressing **Ctrl+Alt+Del**. In the Log On to Windows window, type your user name and password in the text boxes, and then press **Enter**. The Windows 2000 desktop appears on your screen.

2. Click **Start**, point to **Programs**, point to **Microsoft SQL Server**, and then click **Enterprise Manager**. The SQL Server Enterprise Manager window appears.

3. Expand **Microsoft SQL Servers**, and then expand **SQL Server Group**.

4. Right-click your *server_name*, and then click **Properties**. The SQL Server Properties (Configure) dialog box opens.

5. Click the **Security** tab. Under Authentication, click the radio button for **SQL Server and Windows**.

6. Click **OK**. The SQL Server Enterprise Manager dialog box opens indicating that the SQL Server service must be stopped and restarted. Click **Yes**.

7. To minimize Enterprise Manager, click the **Minimize** button in the top-right corner of the window.

To create and verify Windows 2000 users and groups:

1. Click **Start**, and then click **Run**. The Run dialog box opens.

2. To start a Command Prompt window, type **cmd** and then click **OK**. The C:\WINNT\System32\cmd.exe window appears. You may also reach the command prompt by clicking **Start**, pointing to **Programs**, pointing to **Accessories**, and clicking **Command Prompt**.

3. To create the first user, type the following text on the command line, and then press **Enter**:

   net user 228LM_user1 password /add

4. Repeat Step 3 to create another nine users, 228LM_user2 through 228LM_user10.

5. To create a local group, type the following text on the command line, and then press **Enter**:

   net localgroup 228LM_groupA /add

6. To add user accounts to the local group, type the following text on the command line, and then press **Enter**:

   net localgroup 228LM_groupA 228LM_user1 228LM_user2 228LM_user3 /add

7. To create a second local group, type the following text on the command line, and then press **Enter**:

   net localgroup 228LM_groupB /add

8. To add user accounts to the second local group, type the following text on the command line, and then press **Enter**:

   net localgroup 228LM_groupB 228LM_user7 228LM_user8 228LM_user9 /add

9. Click **Start**, point to **Programs**, point to **Administrative Tools**, and then click **Computer Management**. The Computer Management window appears.

10. In the Tree pane, expand **Local Users and Groups**, and then click the **Users** folder. Verify that the 10 user accounts (228LM_user1 through 228LM_user10) were created.

11. In the Tree pane, click the **Groups** folder. Verify that the two group accounts (228LM_groupA and 228LM_groupB) were created.

12. Right-click **228LM_groupA**, and then click **Properties**. The 228LM_groupA Properties dialog box opens. Verify that the 228LM_user1, 228LM_user2, and 228LM_user3 accounts have been made members of this group.

13. Click **Cancel**.

14. Right-click **228LM_groupB**, and then click **Properties**. The 228LM_groupB Properties dialog box opens. Verify that the 228LM_user7, 228LM_user8, and 228LM_user9 accounts have been made members of this group.

15. Click **Cancel**.

16. To close the Computer Management console, click the **Close** button in the top-right corner of the window.

To create a SQL Server login for a Windows group, a second login for a Windows user, and a third login for a non-Windows user, using Enterprise Manger:

1. Return to Enterprise Manager by clicking the **SQL Server Enterprise Manager** button in the taskbar. The SQL Server Enterprise Manager window appears.

2. Expand your *server_name*, and then expand the **Security** folder. Four options—Logins, Server Roles, Linked Servers, and Remote Servers—appear under this folder.

3. Click **Logins**. If you installed SQL Server by following the labs in Chapter 2 of this book, you will see the SQLServerUA Windows user, BUILTIN\Administrators Windows Group, and the sa Standard logins.

4. Right-click **Logins**, and then click **New Login**. The SQL Server Login Properties dialog box opens.

5. After the Name text box, click the browse button (**...**). The SQL Server Login Properties dialog box opens.

6. Click **228LM_groupA**, as shown in Figure 8-1.

7. Click **Add**, and then click **OK**. You are returned to the original SQL Server Login Properties dialog box.

8. Under Authentication, verify that **Windows Authentication** and **Grant access** are selected.

9. Under Defaults, in the Database text box, click the list arrow, and then click **CompanyONE**.

10. Click the **Database Access** tab.

11. Click the box under Permit, next to the CompanyONE database, as shown in Figure 8-2.

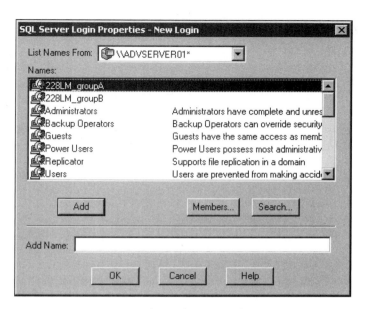

Figure 8-1 Creating a login for a Windows 2000 group

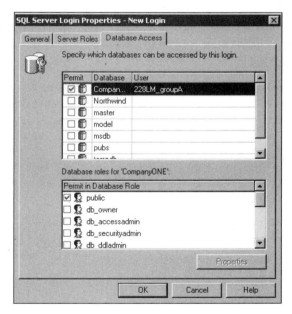

Figure 8-2 Creating a database user from the SQL Server Login Properties dialog box

12. Click **OK**. The SQL Server Login Properties dialog box closes and you are returned to Enterprise Manager.

13. Repeat steps 4 through 11 to create a SQL Server login for the Windows user 228LM_user4.
14. Right-click **Logins**, and then click **New Login**. The SQL Server Login Properties dialog box opens.
15. In the Name text box, type **Outsider1**.
16. Under Authentication, click **SQL Server Authentication**, and then type **OUT1** in the Password text box.

Logins and their passwords for SQL Server are case sensitive only if a case-sensitive sort order was chosen during the SQL Server installation.

17. Under Defaults, in the Database text box, click the list arrow, and then click **CompanyONE**.
18. Click the **Database Access** tab.
19. Click the box under Permit, next to the CompanyONE database.
20. Click **OK**. The Confirm Password dialog box opens.
21. In the Confirm new password text box, type **OUT1**, and then click **OK**.
22. To minimize Enterprise Manager, click the **Minimize** button in the top-right corner of the window.

To create a SQL Server login for a Windows group, a second login for a Windows user, and a third login for a non-Windows user, using T-SQL:

1. Click **Start**, point to **Programs**, point to **Microsoft SQL Server**, and then click **Query Analyzer**. The Connect to SQL Server dialog box opens.
2. Verify that **(local)** is listed in the SQL Server text box, and that the **Windows authentication** radio button is selected, and then click **OK**. The SQL Query Analyzer window appears.
3. If the Object Browser pane is not visible, activate it by pressing **F8**.
4. At the bottom of the Object Browser pane, click the **Templates** tab. The Templates folder is displayed.
5. Expand **Manage Login Role User**. Double-click **Grant Sql Server Access to Windows User or Group**. The syntax of the sp_grantlogin system stored procedure is displayed in the query window.
6. To return to the original blank query window, click **Window** in the menu bar, and then click the first query listed.

Lab 8.1 Creating SQL Server 2000 Logins   153

7. In the query window, type the following text:

    sp_grantlogin '*server_name***\228LM_groupB'**

    and execute the command by pressing **F5**. The message "Granted login access to '*server_name*\228LM_groupB'" appears in the bottom section of the query window.

8. In the query window, edit the previous text to read:

    sp_grantlogin '*server_name***\228LM_user6'**

    and execute the command by pressing **F5**. The message "Granted login access to '*server_name*\228LM_user6'" appears in the bottom section of the query window.

Notice that the sp_grantlogin system stored procedure does not have an option to set the default database. All logins created using this procedure have a default database of master.

9. In the Object Browser pane, on the Templates tab, under the Manage Login Role User folder, double-click **Add Sql Server Login**. The syntax of the sp_addlogin system stored procedure is displayed in the query window.

10. To return to the original query window, click the **Window** menu, and then click the first query listed.

11. In the query window, edit the previous text to read:

    sp_addlogin 'Outsider2','OUT2','CompanyONE'

    and execute the command by pressing **F5**. The message "New login created" appears in the bottom section of the query window.

12. To minimize Query Analyzer, click the **Minimize** button in the top-right corner of the window.

To change the default database using Enterprise Manager and the T-SQL command sp_defaultdb:

1. Return to Enterprise Manager by clicking the **SQL Server Enterprise Manager** button on your taskbar.

2. To refresh the list of logins, right-click **Logins** (under the Security folder in the Tree pane), and then click **Refresh**.

3. Right-click the *server_name***228LM_groupB** login, and then click **Properties**.

4. Under Defaults, in the Database text box, click the list arrow, and then click **CompanyONE**.

5. Click **OK**. The Error dialog box opens indicating that the login just created will not have access to its default database, and asks if you wish to continue. Click **Yes**.

6. To return to Query Analyzer, click the **SQL Query Analyzer** button on your taskbar.

7. In the query window, type the following text:

    sp_defaultdb '*server_name***\228LM_user6','CompanyONE'**

    and execute the command by pressing **F5**. The message "Default database changed" appears in the bottom section of the query window.

8. To close Query Analyzer, click the **Close** button in the top-right corner of the window. The SQL Query Analyzer dialog box opens, asking if you want to save changes.

9. Click **No To All**. You are returned to Enterprise Manager.

10. To close Enterprise Manager, click the **Close** button in the top-right corner of the window.

Certification Objectives

Objectives for Microsoft Exam #70-228: Installing, Configuring, and Administering Microsoft SQL Server 2000 Enterprise Edition:

➤ Configure mixed security modes or Windows Authentication

➤ Create and manage logins

Review Questions

1. Which authentication mode requires all users who need access to the SQL Server to have a Windows 2000 account?
    a. Mixed
    b. SQL Server and Windows
    c. Windows
    d. Account

2. In Enterprise Manager, which folder contains the option Login, through which SQL Server logins can be created?
    a. Databases
    b. Security
    c. Support Services
    d. Accounts

3. Which tab of the SQL Server Login Properties dialog box contains the option to create a database user while creating a new login?
    a. General
    b. Users
    c. Server Roles
    d. Database Access

4. Which of the following T-SQL commands will create a SQL Server login for an existing Windows 2000 account?
   a. sp_grantlogin '*server_name\account_name*'
   b. sp_grantlogin '*server_name\account_name*','*password*','*default_database*'
   c. sp_addlogin '*server_name\account_name*'
   d. sp_addlogin '*server_name\account_name*','*password*','*default_database*'

5. Which of the following T-SQL commands will create a SQL Server login for a user who does not have an existing Windows 2000 account?
   a. sp_grantlogin '*login_name*'
   b. sp_grantlogin '*login_name*','*password*','*default_database*'
   c. sp_addlogin '*login_name*'
   d. sp_addlogin '*login_name*','*password*','*default_database*'

LAB 8.2 CREATING DATABASE USERS

Objectives

The goal of this lab is to create database users for the logins created in Lab 8.1.

Materials Required

This lab will require the following:

- Access to a computer running Windows 2000 Server, Windows 2000 Advanced Server, or Windows 2000 Datacenter Server with SQL Server 2000 installed
- The CompanyONE database, created in Lab 5.2
- The 228LM_groupB, 228LM_user6, and the Outsider2 SQL Server logins, created in Lab 8.1
- The 228LM_user5 Windows 2000 account, created in Lab 8.1

Estimated completion time: **30 minutes**

Activity Background

As you saw in Lab 8.1, database user accounts can be created during the creation of logins when using Enterprise Manager. However, if a login is created using the T-SQL commands sp_grantlogin or sp_addlogin, a database user account is not created simultaneously, and must be done manually. In this lab, you will create a database user account using both Enterprise Manager and the T-SQL command sp_grantdbaccess. Finally, you will create a login and database user account from the Database User Properties dialog box (instead of the SQL Server Login Properties dialog box, as was accomplished in Lab 8.1).

156   **Chapter 8**   Security in SQL Server 2000

ACTIVITY

To create a database user with Enterprise Manager:

1. Boot your computer and log on, if necessary.

2. Click **Start**, point to **Programs**, point to **Microsoft SQL Server**, and then click **Enterprise Manager**. The SQL Server Enterprise Manager window appears.

3. Expand **Microsoft SQL Servers**, expand **SQL Server Group**, and then expand your *server_name*.

4. Expand **Databases**, and then expand the **CompanyONE** database.

5. Right-click **Users**, and then click **New Database User**. The Database User Properties dialog box opens.

6. Click the **Login name** list arrow, and then click *server_name***228LM_groupB** login.

It may be difficult to read the entire login name due to the limited space in the Login name text box. Make a guess, and then click in the User name text box, and scroll over to verify that you have selected the correct login.

7. Click **OK**. The database user is created and you are returned to Enterprise Manager.

To create two database users with Query Analyzer:

1. Click **Start**, point to **Programs**, point to **Microsoft SQL Server**, and then click **Query Analyzer**. The Connect to SQL Server dialog box opens.

2. Verify that **(local)** is listed in the SQL Server text box, and that the **Windows authentication** radio button is selected, and then click **OK**. The SQL Query Analyzer window appears.

3. If the Object Browser pane is not visible, activate it by pressing **F8**.

4. At the bottom of the Object Browser pane, click the **Templates** tab. The Templates folder is displayed.

5. Expand **Manage Login Role User**. Double-click **Grant Database Access to Windows User or SQL Server Login**. The syntax of the sp_grantdbaccess system stored procedure is displayed in the query window.

6. To return to the original blank query window, click the **Window** menu, and then click the first query listed.

7. In the query window, type the following text:

    use CompanyONE
    go
    sp_grantdbaccess '*server_name***\228LM_user6'**

    and execute the command by pressing **F5**. The message "Granted database access to '*server_name*\228LM_user6'" appears in the bottom section of the query window.

8. In the query window, edit the previous text to read:

    use CompanyONE
    go
    sp_grantdbaccess 'Outsider2'

    and execute the command by pressing **F5**. The message "Granted database access to 'Outsider2'" appears in the bottom section of the query window.

9. To close Query Analyzer, click the **Close** button in the top-right corner of the window. The SQL Query Analyzer dialog box opens, asking if you want to save changes.

10. Click **No To All**. You are returned to Enterprise Manager.

11. To refresh the list of database users, right-click **Users** (under the CompanyONE folder in the Tree pane), and then click **Refresh**.

To create a SQL Server login and a database user from the Database User Properties dialog box in Enterprise Manager:

1. Right-click **Users**, and then click **New Database User**. The Database User Properties dialog box opens.

2. Click the **Login name** list arrow, and then click **<new>**, as shown in Figure 8-3. The SQL Server Login Properties dialog box opens.

3. After the Name text box, click the browse button (**...**). The SQL Server Login Properties dialog box opens.

4. Click **228LM_user5**, click **Add**, and then click **OK**. You are returned to the original SQL Server Login Properties dialog box.

5. Under Authentication, verify that **Windows Authentication** and **Grant access** are selected.

6. Under Defaults, in the Database text box, click the list arrow, and then click **CompanyONE**.

7. Click **OK**. The Error dialog box opens indicating that the login just created will not have access to its default database, and asks if you wish to continue.

8. Click **Yes**. You are returned to the Database User Properties dialog box.

9. Click the **Login name** list arrow, and then click *server_name***228LM_user5**.

Figure 8-3 Creating a new SQL Server login from the Database User Properties

10. Click **OK**. The database user is created and you are returned to Enterprise Manager.
11. To refresh the list of database users, right-click **Users** (under the CompanyONE folder in the Tree pane), and then click **Refresh**.

Certification Objectives

Objectives for Microsoft Exam #70-228: Installing, Configuring, and Administering Microsoft SQL Server 2000 Enterprise Edition:

➤ Create and manage database users

Review Questions

1. A database user has access to what?
    a. The database where the user account resides
    b. All databases on the server where the user account resides
    c. All databases on all servers where the user account resides
    d. All databases except master on the server where the user account resides

2. A database user's name can be _____.
    a. the same as the Windows 2000 account name
    b. the same as the SQL Server login name
    c. different from either the Windows 2000 account or SQL Server login name
    d. All of the above

3. Database user names cannot be what?
   a. Symbols
   b. NULL
   c. Numbers
   d. Letters

4. Which of the following T-SQL commands will create a database user for an existing SQL Server login for a Windows 2000 account?
   a. sp_grantdbaccess '*server_name\account_name*'
   b. sp_grantdbaccess '*account_name*'
   c. sp_dbuser '*server_name\account_name*'
   d. sp_dbuser '*account_name*'

5. Which of the following T-SQL commands will create a database user for an existing SQL Server login for a non-Windows account?
   a. sp_grantdbaccess '*server_name\account_name*'
   b. sp_grantdbaccess '*login*'
   c. sp_dbuser '*server_name\account_name*'
   d. sp_dbuser '*login*'

LAB 8.3 CREATING USER-DEFINED DATABASE ROLES

Objectives

The goal of this lab is to view the fixed server roles, the fixed database roles, and to create a user-defined database role using Enterprise Manager and the T-SQL commands sp_addrole and sp_addrolemember.

Materials Required

This lab will require the following:

➤ Access to a computer running Windows 2000 Server, Windows 2000 Advanced Server, or Windows 2000 Datacenter Server with SQL Server 2000 installed

➤ The CompanyONE database, created in Lab 5.2

➤ The 228LM_user4, 228LM_user5, and the 228LM_user6 database users in the CompanyONE database, created in Lab 8.2

➤ The Outsider1 and Outsider2 database users in the CompanyONE database, created in Lab 8.2

160 Chapter 8 Security in SQL Server 2000

Estimated completion time: **20 minutes**

Activity Background

Similar to Windows 2000 groups, database roles allow you to group database users together into a single unit. Windows 2000 groups are the preferred choice, but are sometimes not available. For example, consider the situation in which a few people from several different departments are needed for a project. Another possibility is that you, as the SQL database administrator, do not have the appropriate rights to create Windows 2000 groups. Whatever the reason, SQL Server roles simplify your security environment because you apply permissions only once to the role, rather than to each user.

ACTIVITY

To view the fixed server and fixed database roles:

1. Boot your computer and log on, if necessary.

2. Click **Start**, point to **Programs**, point to **Microsoft SQL Server**, and then click **Enterprise Manager**. The SQL Server Enterprise Manager window appears.

3. Expand **Microsoft SQL Servers**, expand **SQL Server Group**, and then expand your *server_name*.

4. Expand **Security**, and then click **Server Roles**. The eight fixed server roles are displayed on the right side of the screen.

5. In the Tree pane, expand **Databases**, expand the **CompanyONE** database, and then click **Roles**. The 10 fixed database roles are displayed on the right side of the screen.

To create a user-defined role using Enterprise Manager:

1. In the Tree pane, right-click **Roles**, and then click **New Database Role**. The Database Role Properties dialog box opens.

2. In the Name text box, type **228LM_role**.

3. Under Database role type, verify that **Standard role** is selected, and then click **Add**. The Add Role Members dialog box opens.

4. Click the **228LM_user4**, *server_name***228LM_user5**, and *server_name***228LM_user6** users, as shown in Figure 8-4, and then click **OK**. You are returned to the Database Role Properties dialog box.

A user name may or may not be preceded by a server name, depending on how the user was created (T-SQL commands versus Enterprise Manager).

5. Click **OK**. The role is created and you are returned to Enterprise Manager.

Figure 8-4 Adding database users to a user-defined database role

To create a user-defined database role using T-SQL commands:

1. Click **Start**, point to **Programs**, point to **Microsoft SQL Server**, and then click **Query Analyzer**. The Connect to SQL Server dialog box opens.

2. Verify that **(local)** is listed in the SQL Server text box, and that the **Windows authentication** radio button is selected, and then click **OK**. The SQL Query Analyzer window appears.

3. In the query window, type the following text:

   use CompanyONE
   go
   sp_addrole 'Outsiders'

   and execute the command by pressing **F5**. The message "New role added" appears in the bottom section of the query window.

4. If the Object Browser pane is not visible, activate it by pressing **F8**.

5. At the bottom of the Object Browser pane, click the **Templates** tab. The Templates folder is displayed.

6. Expand **Manage Login Role User**. Double-click **Add User to Database Role**. The syntax of the sp_addrolemember system stored procedure is displayed in the query window.

7. To return to the original blank query window, click the **Window** menu, and then click the first query listed.

8. In the query window, edit the previous text to read:

   use CompanyONE
   go
   sp_addrolemember 'Outsiders', 'Outsider1'
   go
   ap_addrolemember 'Outsiders','Outsider2'

   and execute the command by pressing **F5**. The messages "'Outsider1' added to role 'Outsiders'" and "'Outsider2' added to role 'Outsiders'" appear in the bottom section of the query window.

9. To close Query Analyzer, click the **Close** button in the top-right corner of the window. The SQL Query Analyzer dialog box opens, asking if you want to save changes.

10. Click **No To All**. You are returned to Enterprise Manager.

11. To refresh the list of roles, right-click **Roles** (under the CompanyONE folder in the Tree pane), and then click **Refresh**.

12. To close Enterprise Manager, click the **Close** button in the top-right corner of the window.

Certification Objectives

Objectives for Microsoft Exam #70-228: Installing, Configuring, and Administering Microsoft SQL Server 2000 Enterprise Edition:

➤ Create and manage security roles; roles include application, database and server

➤ Create roles to manage database security

Review Questions

1. Which fixed server role can manage logins for the server?
   a. Security Administrators
   b. Server Administrators
   c. Setup Administrators
   d. System Administrators

2. Which of the following is true of a fixed database role?
   a. It can be renamed
   b. It can be deleted
   c. The permissions assigned to it can be changed
   d. Database users can be added to it

3. What type of accounts can be members of a database role?
   a. Windows 2000 accounts
   b. SQL Server logins

c. Database users
d. All of the above

4. Which of the following T-SQL commands will create a database role for the current database?
   a. sp_addrole '*database_name\role_name*'
   b. sp_addrole '*role_name*'
   c. sp_addrolemember '*database_name\role_name*'
   d. sp_addrolemember '*role_name*'

5. Which of the following T-SQL commands will add a database user to a database role for the current database?
   a. sp_addrole '*role_name*','*user_name*'
   b. sp_addrole '*user_name*'
   c. sp_addrolemember '*role_name*','*user_name*'
   d. sp_addrolemember '*user_name*'

LAB 8.4 SETTING STATEMENT AND OBJECT PERMISSIONS

Objectives

The goal of this lab is to set statement and object permissions in the CompanyONE database.

Materials Required

This lab will require the following:

➤ Access to a computer running Windows 2000 Server, Windows 2000 Advanced Server, or Windows 2000 Datacenter Server with SQL Server 2000 installed

➤ The CompanyONE database, created in Lab 5.2; including the C1Employee and C1OfficeLocation tables, created in Lab 5.5

➤ The 228LM_groupA and 228LM_groupB database users in the CompanyONE database, created in Lab 8.2

➤ The 228LM_role database role in the CompanyONE database, created in Lab 8.3

Estimated completion time: **20 minutes**

Activity Background

Now that you have created the SQL Server logins and the database users and roles, you can secure your database with permissions. Statement permissions allow you to decide who can execute various T-SQL statements (or the equivalent operation in Enterprise Manager) such as CREATE TABLE. Object permissions indicate which users can access, add, update, or delete data. When setting permissions, you have three choices: Grant, Deny, and Revoke. Grant and Deny are obvious; Revoke is a little trickier. Revoke removes a specific permission from a user, but allows them to inherit that permission through membership in a Windows 2000 group or database role. In this activity, you will set both Statement and Object permissions using Enterprise Manager and the T-SQL commands GRANT and DENY.

ACTIVITY

To set statement permissions for the 228LM_groupA database user with Enterprise Manager:

1. Boot your computer and log on, if necessary.
2. Click **Start**, point to **Programs**, point to **Microsoft SQL Server**, and then click **Enterprise Manager**. The SQL Server Enterprise Manager window appears.
3. Expand **Microsoft SQL Servers**, expand **SQL Server Group**, and then expand your *server_name*.
4. Expand **Databases**, right-click the **CompanyONE** database, and then click **Properties**. The CompanyONE Properties dialog box opens.
5. Click the **Permissions** tab.
6. Click the box under Create Table for the 228LM_groupA user, to place a green check in the box.

Both Object and Statement permissions boxes are three-way toggles. Clicking once in a box produces a green check (Grant), clicking twice produces a red X (Deny), and clicking three times produces a blank box (Revoke). If you make a mistake, just keep clicking until you get the results you require.

7. Click the box under Create View twice for the 228LM_groupA user, to place a red X in the box, as shown in Figure 8-5.
8. Click **OK**. You are returned to Enterprise Manager.

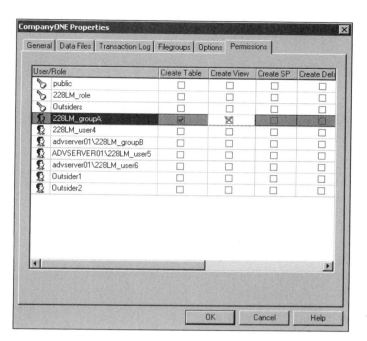

Figure 8-5 Granting and denying permissions

To set object permissions for the 228LM_groupB database user and the 228LM_role database role, using Enterprise Manager:

1. Expand the **CompanyONE** database, and then click **Tables**. The System and User tables are displayed on the right side of the window.
2. Right-click the **C1Employee** table, and then click **Properties**. The Table Properties dialog box opens.
3. Click **Permissions**. The Object Properties dialog box opens.
4. Click the box in the SELECT column for the 228LM_role database role.
5. Click the boxes in the SELECT, INSERT, UPDATE, and DELETE columns for the 228LM_groupB database user, as shown in Figure 8-6, and then click **Apply**.
6. Click the Object list arrow, and then click the **C1OfficeLocation** table.
7. Click the boxes in the SELECT and INSERT columns for the 228LM_groupB database user.
8. Click **OK** twice. You are returned to Enterprise Manager.
9. To close Enterprise Manager, click the **Close** button in the top-right corner of the window.

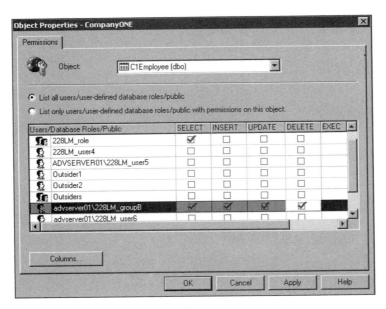

Figure 8-6 Granting statement permissions

To set permissions using T-SQL:

1. Click **Start**, point to **Programs**, point to **Microsoft SQL Server**, and then click **Query Analyzer**. The Connect to SQL Server dialog box opens.

2. Verify that **(local)** is listed in the SQL Server text box, and that the **Windows authentication** radio button is selected, and then click **OK**. The SQL Query Analyzer window appears.

3. In the query window, type the following text:

   use CompanyONE
   go
   grant create table to Outsider1

   and execute the command by pressing **F5**. The message "The command(s) completed successfully." appears in the bottom section of the query window.

4. In the query window, edit the previous text to read:

   use CompanyONE
   go
   grant all on C1Employee to Outsider2

   and execute the command by pressing **F5**. The message "The command(s) completed successfully." appears in the bottom section of the query window.

5. In the query window, edit the previous text to read:

   use CompanyONE
   go
   deny delete on C1Employee to Outsider2

and execute the command by pressing **F5**. The message "The command(s) completed successfully." appears in the bottom section of the query window.

6. To close Query Analyzer, click the **Close** button in the top-right corner of the window. The SQL Query Analyzer dialog box opens, asking if you want to save changes.

7. Click **No To All**.

Certification Objectives

Objectives for Microsoft Exam #70-228: Installing, Configuring, and Administering Microsoft SQL Server 2000 Enterprise Edition:

➤ Set permissions in a database; considerations include object permissions, object ownership, and statement permissions

Review Questions

1. Which of the following is a statement permission?
   a. SELECT
   b. INSERT
   c. UPDATE
   d. CREATE TABLE

2. Which of the following is an object permission?
   a. DELETE
   b. CREATE VIEW
   c. CREATE DEFAULT
   d. BACKUP DATABASE

3. Statement and object permissions can be set for _____.
   a. Windows 2000 accounts
   b. SQL Server logins
   c. database users
   d. database users and database roles

4. User1 is a database user in the TESTDB database, and is a member of Group1, which itself is also a database user. Both User1 and Group1 are granted SELECT, INSERT, UPDATE, and DELETE object permissions on a table in the TESTDB database. What effect will revoking User1's permissions have on that user's access to the table?
   a. User1 will have no access to the table.
   b. User1 will have the SELECT permission to the table.
   c. User1 will have the SELECT, INSERT, UPDATE, and DELETE permissions to the table.
   d. User1 will be removed from the group Group1.

5. User1 is a database user in the TESTDB database, and is a member of Group1, which itself is also a database user. Both User1 and Group1 are granted SELECT, INSERT, UPDATE, and DELETE object permissions on a table in the TESTDB database. What effect will denying User1's permissions have on that user's access to the table?
   a. User1 will have no access to the table.
   b. User1 will have the SELECT permission to the table.
   c. User1 will have the SELECT, INSERT, UPDATE, and DELETE permissions to the table.
   d. User1 will be removed from the group Group1.

LAB 8.5 TESTING LOGINS, USERS, ROLES, AND PERMISSIONS

Objectives

The goal of this lab is to test the SQL Server logins, database users, database roles, and permissions created or set in Labs 8.1, 8.2, 8.3, and 8.4.

Materials Required

This lab will require the following:

➤ Access to a computer running Windows 2000 Server, Windows 2000 Advanced Server, or Windows 2000 Datacenter Server with SQL Server 2000 installed

➤ The CompanyONE database, created in Lab 5.2; including the C1Employee and C1OfficeLocation tables, created in Lab 5.5

➤ The 228LM_user10 Windows 2000 user account, created in Lab 8.1

➤ The 228LM_groupA and 228LM_groupB database users in the CompanyONE database, created in Lab 8.2

➤ The 228LM_role database role in the CompanyONE database, created in Lab 8.3

➤ The statement and object permissions set in Lab 8.4

Estimated completion time: **60 minutes**

Activity Background

Now that you have set up your secure environment, defined which Windows 2000 accounts can have access to your server, and set the appropriate permissions for the database users and roles, you must test everything. Only after thorough testing can you allow users to connect to and begin using the database.

Lab 8.5 Testing Logins, Users, Roles, and Permissions 169

ACTIVITY

To verify that 228LM_user10 does not have access to the SQL Server:

1. Boot your computer and log on, if necessary.

2. Click **Start**, and then click **Shut Down**. The Shut Down Windows dialog box opens.

3. Click the list arrow, click **Log off** *account_name*, and then click **OK**. The Welcome to Windows screen appears.

4. Press **Ctrl+Alt+Del**. The Log On to Windows dialog box opens.

5. In the User name text box type **228LM_user10**, in the Password text box type **password**; and then click **OK**. The Windows 2000 desktop appears.

6. Click **Start**, point to **Programs**, point to **Microsoft SQL Server**, and then click **Enterprise Manager**. The SQL Server Enterprise Manager window appears.

7. Expand **Microsoft SQL Servers**, expand **SQL Server Group**, and then expand your *server_name*. The SQL Server Enterprise Manager dialog box opens, indicating that a connection could not be established to the server, and that the login failed.

228LM_user10 is not a member of either 228LM_groupA or 228LM_groupB, and was not granted access to the SQL Server.

8. Click **OK**.

9. To close Enterprise Manager, click the **Close** button in the top-right corner of the window.

10. Click **Start**, and then click **Shut Down**. The Shut Down Windows dialog box opens.

11. Click the list arrow, click **Log off 228LM_user10**, and then click **OK**. The Welcome to Windows screen appears.

To verify that 228LM_user1 has no object permissions, and has the statement permissions to create tables:

1. Press **Ctrl+Alt+Del**. The Log On to Windows dialog box opens.

2. In the User name text box type **228LM_user1**, and in the Password text box type **password**; and then click **OK**. The Windows 2000 desktop appears.

3. Click **Start**, point to **Programs**, point to **Microsoft SQL Server**, and then click **Enterprise Manager**. The SQL Server Enterprise Manager window appears.

4. Expand **Microsoft SQL Servers**, expand **SQL Server Group**, and then expand your *server_name*.

5. Expand **Databases**, expand the **CompanyONE** database, and then click **Tables**. The System and User tables are displayed on the right side of the window.

6. In the list of tables, right-click **C1Employee**, point to **Open Table**, and then click **Return all rows**. The SQL Server Enterprise Manager dialog box opens, indicating that an unexpected error happened, and that you might not have the needed permission, as shown in Figure 8-7.

Figure 8-7 The SQL Server Enterprise Manager dialog box

7. Click **OK**. You are returned to Enterprise Manager.

8. In the Tree pane, right-click **Tables**, and then click **New Table**.

9. As Table Designer is launching, the SQL Server Enterprise Manager dialog box opens, indicating that you are not logged on as the database owner or system administrator. Click **OK**.

10. Under Column Name, enter **C1Col1**, and then press **Tab** four times to move the cursor to the Column Name field of the second row, as shown in Figure 8-8. SQL Server Table Designer enters the defaults of char(10) and allows nulls for you.

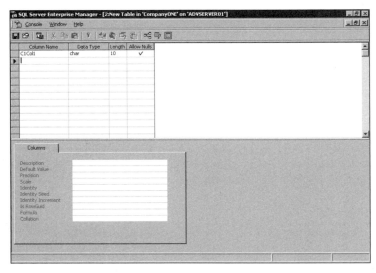

Figure 8-8 Accepting the defaults in the Table Designer window

Lab 8.5 Testing Logins, Users, Roles, and Permissions 171

11. In the Column Name for the second row, enter **C1Col2**, and then press **Tab** four times to again accept the defaults and move to the new row.

12. In the toolbar, click the **Save** button. The Choose Name dialog box opens.

13. Enter **C1Test**, and then click **OK**.

14. To close the Table Designer window, click the lower of the two **Close** buttons in the top-right corner of the window.

15. To close Enterprise Manager, click the **Close** button in the top-right corner of the window.

16. Click **Start**, and then click **Shut Down**. The Shut Down Windows dialog box opens.

17. Click the list arrow, click **Log off 228LM_user1**, and then click **OK**. The Welcome to Windows screen appears.

To verify that 228LM_user7 has the SELECT and INSERT permissions on the C1OfficeLocation table, and the SELECT, INSERT, UPDATE, and DELETE permissions on the C1Employee table:

1. Press **Ctrl+Alt+Del**. The Log On to Windows dialog box opens.

2. In the User name text box type **228LM_user7**, and in the Password text box type **password**; and then click **OK**. The Windows 2000 desktop appears.

3. Click **Start**, point to **Programs**, point to **Microsoft SQL Server**, and then click **Enterprise Manager**. The SQL Server Enterprise Manager window appears.

4. Expand **Microsoft SQL Servers**, expand **SQL Server Group**, and then expand your *server_name*.

5. Expand **Databases**, expand the **CompanyONE** database, and then click **Tables**. The System an User tables are displayed on the right side of the window.

6. In the list of tables, right-click **C1OfficeLocation**, point to **Open Table**, and then click **Return all rows**.

7. Enter your business address into the table, using the digit **1** for the location.

8. Change the OfficeState to **XX**.

9. To close the Data in Table window, click the lower of the two **Close** buttons in the top-right corner of the window. The SQL Server Enterprise Manager dialog box opens, indicating that the UPDATE permission is denied, as shown in Figure 8-9.

Chapter 8 Security in SQL Server 2000

Figure 8-9 The SQL Server Enterprise Manager dialog box

10. Click **OK**.

11. In the list of tables, right-click **C1Employee**, point to **Open Table**, and then click **Return all rows**.

12. Enter your name, social security number, and home address into the table, using the digit **1** for the location.

13. Change your social security number to **999999999**.

14. Right-click the gray box to the left of your last name (to select the entire row), and then click **Delete**. The SQL Server Enterprise Manager dialog box opens, indicating that you are about to delete one row.

15. Click **Yes**.

16. To close the Data in Table window, click the lower of the two **Close** buttons in the top-right corner of the window.

17. To close Enterprise Manager, click the **Close** button in the top-right corner of the window.

18. Click **Start**, and then click **Shut Down**. The Shut Down Windows dialog box opens.

19. Click the list arrow, click **Log off 228LM_user7**, and then click **OK**. The Welcome to Windows screen appears.

To verify that the 228LM_user4 database user has the SELECT permission on the C1Employee table only:

1. Press **Ctrl+Alt+Del**. The Log On to Windows dialog box opens.

2. In the User name text box type **228LM_user4**, and in the Password text box type **password**; and then click **OK**. The Windows 2000 desktop appears.

3. Click **Start**, point to **Programs**, point to **Microsoft SQL Server**, and then click **Enterprise Manager**. The SQL Server Enterprise Manager window appears.

4. Expand **Microsoft SQL Servers**, expand **SQL Server Group**, and then expand your *server_name*.

5. Expand **Databases**, expand the **CompanyONE** database, and then click **Tables**. The System and User tables are displayed on the right side of the window.

6. In the list of tables, right-click **C1Employee**, point to **Open Table**, and then click **Return all rows**. The table is opened.

7. To close the Data in Table window, click the lower of the two **Close** buttons in the top-right corner of the window.

8. In the list of tables, right-click **C1OfficeLocation**, point to **Open Table**, and then click **Return all rows**. The SQL Server Enterprise Manager dialog box opens, indicating that an unexpected error occurred, and you might not have the needed permission.

9. Click **OK**. You are returned to Enterprise Manager.

10. To close Enterprise Manager, click the **Close** button in the top-right corner of the window.

11. Click **Start**, and then click **Shut Down**. The Shut Down Windows dialog box opens.

12. Click the list arrow, click **Log off 228LM_user4**, and then click **OK**. The Welcome to Windows screen appears.

Review Questions

1. You are the administrator of a SQL Server 2000 computer. The server contains seven databases that provide data to several company client/server applications. A different user maintains each database. You must configure server and database permissions so that each user who maintains a database has full permissions on that database. What should you do?
   a. Create a domain user group for all users, add a login for the domain user group, and then add the login to the sysadmin server role.
   b. Create a domain user group for all users, add a login for the domain user group, map the login to a database user in each database, and then add all database users to the db_owner database role in each database.
   c. Create a login for each user's domain user account, map each login to a database user in the appropriate databases, and then add the database users to the db_owner database role in each database.
   d. Create a login for each user's domain user account, and then add the logins to the dbcreator server role.

2. You have three Windows domain users groups defined. Each group must be able to read and modify their own data but not another group's data. How should you configure the database so that it meets these requirements, and results in less administration time and consumption of server resources? (Choose all that apply.)
   a. Create a database for each group.
   b. Create a database for all groups.
   c. Create a Windows-Authenticated login for each group.
   d. Map each domain users group to the db_datareader and db_datawriter database roles.

174   Chapter 8   Security in SQL Server 2000

3. A user named Robin needs to create new tables in a database named CorpSales, but should not have access to other databases on the server. You create a SQL Server login for Robin. She reports that she can log in to the server but is unable to access the CorpSales database. What should you do?
   a. Create a new database user in the CorpSales database, map the database user to Robin's login, and then grant CREATE TABLE permissions to the database user.
   b. Create a new database role in the CorpSales database, add Robin's login as a member of the role, and then grant CREATE TABLE permissions to the database role.
   c. Change the server's authentication mode to Windows Authentication, and then add Robin's login to the processadmin server role on the server.

4. You are the administrator of a SQL Server 2000 computer that stores confidential company information. Company policy requires that every action and change of permission on the server be logged. Policy also requires that the server can run only when logging is enabled. You need to configure the server to comply with this policy. What should you do?
   a. Use SQL Profiler to capture security events and audit events, and make sure that file rollover is enabled.
   b. On the Security tab of the Server Properties dialog box, set the Audit Level to All.
   c. Configure the server to use Windows Authentication mode, and make sure the Windows Security Log does not overwrite events.
   d. Set the C2 audit mode option to 1, and then restart the MSSQLServer service.

5. You are the administrator of a SQL Server 2000 computer. The server is a member of a Windows NT domain and is configured for Windows Authentication mode. The server contains a database that stores contact information for public officials in your region. These officials must access the database by means of the Internet by using the SQL Server Guest login. However, some users report that they cannot connect to the server by means of the Internet. You need to allow anyone access to the server by means of the Internet. What should you do?
   a. Assign the Guest login a blank password.
   b. Delete the Guest login and create a new login that is mapped to the Guest domain user account.
   c. Create a database user named Anonymous and assign the user the appropriate database permissions.
   d. Configure the server for Mixed mode authentication.

CHAPTER NINE

EXTRACTING AND TRANSFORMING DATA WITH SQL SERVER 2000

Labs included in this chapter

- ➤ Lab 9.1 Loading Data With BULK INSERT
- ➤ Lab 9.2 Using the Data Transformation Services
- ➤ Lab 9.3 Setting up Merge Replication
- ➤ Lab 9.4 Supporting XML in Microsoft SQL Server 2000

Microsoft MCSE Exam #70-228 Objectives	
Objective	Lab
Import and export data; methods include the Bulk Insert task, the bulk copy program, Data Transformation Services (DTS), and heterogeneous queries	9.1, 9.2
Configure, maintain, and troubleshoot replication services	9.3

LAB 9.1 LOADING DATA WITH BULK INSERT

Objectives

The goal of this lab is to become familiar with the BULK INSERT command. In order to execute the command, you will need to make a given user a member of the sysadmin or bulkadmin role. The bulkadmin role did not exist until SQL Server 2000.

Materials Required

This lab will require the following:

➤ Access to a computer running Windows 2000 Server, Windows 2000 Advanced Server, or Windows 2000 Datacenter Server with SQL Server 2000 installed

➤ The Investors.txt student file (This file accompanies *MCSE Guide to SQL Server 2000 Administration*, by Mathew Raftree, Course Technology, 2002, 0-619-03553-6, and can be downloaded from the Student Downloads section of the Course Technology Web site at *www.course.com*.)

Estimated completion time: **20 minutes**

Activity Background

In this lab, you will learn how to load data using the BULK INSERT command. First, you will create a login to use with the command. The necessary permissions will be applied to the login. Rather than assigning the user to the sysadmin role, you will give the user bulkadmin rights. This will ensure that the user can only execute the BULK INSERT command but not perform administration commands.

ACTIVITY

1. Boot your computer and log on, if necessary.

2. Click **Start**, point to **Programs**, point to **Microsoft SQL Server**, and then click **Books Online**. The SQL Server Books Online window appears.

3. In the Navigation pane, click the **Index** tab. Type **BULK INSERT** in the keyword text box, and double-click the **BULK INSERT (described)** topic.

4. This topic describes in detail the BULK INSERT command's syntax. Read through the information displayed.

5. To close Books Online, click the **Close** button in the top-right corner of the window.

6. Click **Start**, point to **Programs**, point to **Microsoft SQL Server**, and then click **Enterprise Manager**. The SQL Server Enterprise Manager window appears.

7. Expand **Microsoft SQL Servers**, expand **SQL Server Group**, and then expand your *server_name*.
8. Left-click **Security** to expand the **Security Group**.
9. Right-click **Logins**, and then select **New Login**. The SQL Server Login Properties dialog box opens.
10. For the Name option, type **BulkUser**. Click the **SQL Server Authentication** radio button, and then type the password **example** as shown in Figure 9-1. (The password will appear as asterisks for security purposes.)

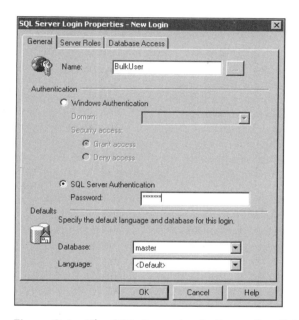

Figure 9-1 The SQL Server Login Properties dialog box

11. Click the **Server Roles** tab, and then click the **Bulk Insert Administrators** role.
12. Click the **Database Access** tab. In the upper pane, click the **Permit** check box next to the **Northwind** database. In the lower pane, click the **db_owner** role, and verify that **public** is already selected.
13. Complete adding the account by clicking **OK**, and retype the password (example) when prompted.
14. To close Enterprise Manager, click the **Close** button in the top-right corner of the window.
15. Click **Start**, point to **Programs**, point to **Microsoft SQL Server**, and then click **Query Analyzer**.

16. Verify that **(local)** is listed in the SQL Server text box and that the **SQL Server authentication** radio button is selected. Type the login name **BulkUser** and the password **example**, and then click **OK**. The SQL Query Analyzer window appears.

17. Select the **Northwind** database from the Database list box.

18. If the investors table has not yet been created, type the following statement in the query window to create the necessary table:

    CREATE TABLE [Investors] (
    FirstName varchar (25) NULL,
    LastName varchar (25) NULL,
    Amount varchar (25) NULL,
    PhoneNumber varchar (25) NULL)

    Execute the command by pressing **F5**.

19. To load data into the table, type the following text in the query window:
    bulk insert Northwind.dbo.investors
        from '*path*\Investors.txt'
        with (batchsize = 10)
    where *path* is the path where you have located the "Investors.txt" student file. Press **F5** to execute the query.

20. Verify that the data is in the table by typing the following query in the query window:
    select * from Northwind.dbo.investors
    and then press **F5** to execute the query.

21. To close Query Analyzer, click the **Close** button in the top-right corner of the window. When prompted to save the query click **No To All**.

Certification Objectives

Objectives for Microsoft Exam #70-228: Installing, Configuring, and Administering Microsoft SQL Server 2000 Enterprise Edition:

➤ Import and export data; methods include the Bulk Insert task, the bulk copy program, Data Transformation Services (DTS), and heterogeneous queries

Review Questions

1. What server role must a user be a member of to execute the BULK INSERT command?
    a. serveradmin
    b. sysadminister
    c. securityadmin
    d. bulkadmin

2. Which keyword is used to denote a new row in the BULK INSERT command?
   a. KEEPIDENTITY
   b. FIELDTERMINATOR
   c. ROWTERMINATOR
   d. DATAFILETYPE

3. Which keyword is used to denote a new column in the BULK INSERT command?
   a. KEEPIDENTITY
   b. FIELDTERMINATOR
   c. ROWTERMINATOR
   d. DATAFILETYPE

4. What keyword in the BULK INSERT command can be used to specify how many records will be committed at a time?
   a. TABLOCK
   b. BATCHSIZE
   c. ROWTERMINATOR
   d. FIRSTROW

5. What keyword in the BULK INSERT command can be used to work around the situation in which you have a header record with the column names in your file?
   a. TABLOCK
   b. BATCHSIZE
   c. ROWTERMINATOR
   d. FIRSTROW

LAB 9.2 USING THE DATA TRANSFORMATION SERVICES

Objectives

The goal of this lab to learn about Data Transformation Services. You will be transferring all the vegetarian products from a SQL Server table in the Northwind database to the pubs database.

Materials Required

This lab will require the following:

➤ Access to a computer running Windows 2000 Server, Windows 2000 Advanced Server, or Windows 2000 Datacenter Server with SQL Server 2000 installed

180 Chapter 9 Extracting and Transforming Data with SQL Server 2000

Estimated completion time: **20 minutes**

Activity

1. Boot your computer and log on, if necessary.

2. Click **Start**, point to **Programs**, point to **Microsoft SQL Server**, and then click **Books Online**. The SQL Server Books Online window appears.

3. In the Navigation pane, click the **Search** tab. Type **"DTS Tasks"** (including the quotes) in the search text box, and select the **DTS Tasks** topic.

4. This topic describes the purpose of each of the DTS tasks. Read through the information displayed.

5. To close Books Online, click the **Close** button in the top-right corner of the window.

6. Click **Start**, point to **Programs**, point to **Microsoft SQL Server**, and then click **Enterprise Manager**. The SQL Server Enterprise Manager window appears.

7. Expand **Microsoft SQL Servers**, expand **SQL Server Group**, and then expand your *server_name*.

8. Right-click the **Data Transformation Services** folder, and then select **New Package**. The DTS Designer window appears.

9. Click the **Connection** menu, and then select **Microsoft OLE DB Provider for SQL Server**. The Connection Properties dialog box opens.

10. In the New connection text box, type **Source Connection**. Verify that **(local)** is listed in the Server text box and that the **Use Windows Authentication** radio button is selected. Click the Database list arrow, and then select the **Northwind** database as shown in Figure 9-2. To close the Connection Properties dialog box and save the properties, click **OK**.

11. Click the **Connection** menu, and then select **Microsoft OLE DB Provider for SQL Server**. The Connection Properties dialog box opens.

12. In the New connection text box, type **Destination Connection**. Verify that **(local)** is selected in the Server text box and that the **Use Windows Authentication** radio button is selected, and then click **OK**. Click the Database list arrow, and then select **pubs**. To close the Connection Properties dialog box and save the properties, click **OK**.

13. Click the **Task** menu, and then click **Transform Data Task**. Left-click the **Source Connection** task you created in Step 10, and then left-click **Destination Connection**. This creates an arrow pointing to the Destination Connection task.

14. Double-click the arrow connecting the two tasks. The Transform Data Task Properties dialog box opens.

Lab 9.2 Using the Data Transformation Services 181

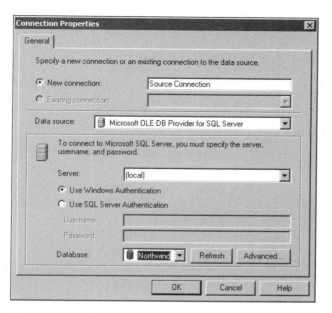

Figure 9-2 The Connection Properties dialog box

15. Click the **Source** tab, and then type **Transform Vegetarian Products** in the Description text box.

16. Click the SQL Query radio button, and then type the following text in the query box:

    **select * from Products
    where CategoryID IN (1,2,3,5)**

    Press **F5** to execute the query.

17. Click the **Destination** tab, and then click **Create** (to the right of the Table name list arrow). The Create Destination Table dialog box opens.

18. Change the name of the table from [New Table] to **[VegetarianProducts]** in the first line of the CREATE TABLE statement, and then click **OK**. You are returned to the Transform Data Task Properties dialog box.

19. Click the **Transformations** tab, and save the task's properties by clicking **OK**.

20. Click the **Package** menu, and then click **Save**. The Save DTS Package dialog box opens. Type **Transform Vegetarian Products** in the Package name text box. Verify that **SQL Server** is selected in the Location list. Verify that **(local)** or your *server_name* is selected in the Server text box and that the **Use Windows Authentication** radio button is selected, as shown in Figure 9-3, and then click **OK**.

21. Click the **Package** menu, and then click **Execute**. Click **OK** when the Package Execution Results dialog box opens confirming that the package was successfully completed. Click **Done** to confirm the execution.

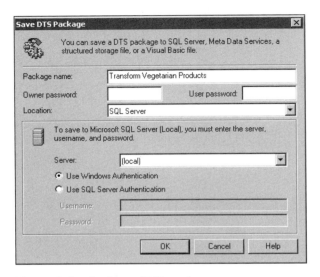

Figure 9-3 Saving a DTS package

22. To close the Package Designer window, click the **Close** button in the top-right corner of the window. You are returned to the SQL Server Enterprise Manager window.

23. To close Enterprise Manager, click the **Close** button in the top-right corner of the window.

Certification Objectives

Objectives for Microsoft Exam #70-228: Installing, Configuring, and Administering Microsoft SQL Server 2000 Enterprise Edition:

➤ Import and export data; methods include the Bulk Insert task, the bulk copy program, Data Transformation Services (DTS), and heterogeneous queries

Review Questions

1. Where do you launch DTS Designer?
    a. From the Start menu
    b. From inside Enterprise Manager
    c. By executing the isql utility
    d. From Query Analyzer

2. What task allows you to copy data from one location to another?
    a. Execute Process task
    b. Execute Package task
    c. Transform Data task
    d. Dynamic Properties task

3. From what tab in the Transform Data task do you specify that you would like to transform a subset amount of data with a WHERE clause?
    a. Source
    b. Destination
    c. Transformations
    d. Options

4. By selecting SQL Server in the Location list when saving the package, where does this save the package?
    a. In Meta Data Services
    b. VB file
    c. Locally
    d. COM-structured file

5. From what menu can you execute a package?
    a. Package
    b. Execute
    c. Task
    d. Connection

LAB 9.3 SETTING UP MERGE REPLICATION

Objectives

The goal of this lab is to become familiar with SQL Server 2000 replication by setting up SQL Server Merge replication.

Materials Required

This lab will require the following:

➤ Access to a computer running Windows 2000 Server, Windows 2000 Advanced Server, or Windows 2000 Datacenter Server with SQL Server 2000 installed

➤ The SQLServerUA user account, created in Lab 2.1

Estimated completion time: **30 minutes**

Activity Background

In this lab, you will set up SQL Server Merge replication. Because you might not have multiple servers available, you will set up one server as the Publisher, Distributor, and Subscriber. Before you begin with the replication part of the lab, you must confirm that

184   Chapter 9   Extracting and Transforming Data with SQL Server 2000

the SQL Server Agent service (SQLSERVERAGENT) is not being started with the local system account and start the service. When you complete the replication activity, you will stop the SQL Server Agent service in preparation for the labs in Chapter 10.

Activity

1. Boot your computer and log on, if necessary.

2. Click **Start**, point to **Programs**, point to **Administrative Tools**, and then click **Services**. The Services window appears.

3. Navigate through the services and double-click **SQLSERVERAGENT**. The SQLSERVERAGENT Properties (Local Computer) window appears. Click the **Startup type** list arrow and select **Automatic**, if necessary.

4. Click the **Log On** tab, and verify that the **This account** option is selected. If the SQLServerUA account is not listed in the account text box, click **Browse**. The Select User dialog box opens. Click the **SQLServerUA** account, and then click **OK**. In the Password and Confirm password text boxes, type the password **SQLServerPWD**, and then click **OK**. The Shared Folders dialog box opens indicating that the new login name will not take effect until you stop and restart the service. Click **OK**. You are returned to the Services window.

5. Right-click the **SQLSERVERAGENT** service, and then click **Start**. (If the service is already started, click **Stop**, and then right-click the **SQLSERVERAGENT** service again and click **Start**).

The SQL Server Agent service is covered in more detail in Chapter 10.

6. Close the Services window by clicking the **Close** button in the top-right corner of the window.

7. Click **Start**, point to **Programs**, point to **Microsoft SQL Server**, and then click **Enterprise Manager**. The SQL Server Enterprise Manager window appears.

8. Expand **Microsoft SQL Servers**, expand **SQL Server Group**, and click your *server_name*.

9. Click the **Tools** menu, point to **Replication**, and then click **Configure Publishing, Subscribers, and Distribution**. The Configure Publishing and Distribution Wizard starts. Click **Next**. The Select Distributor screen appears.

10. Verify that the **Make *server_name* its own Distributor** radio button is selected, and then click **Next**. The Specify Snapshot Folder screen appears.

11. Use the default location. Click **Next**. If the SQL Server Enterprise Manager dialog box opens asking you to confirm the path, click **Yes**.

12. In the Customize the Configuration screen, select the No, **use the default settings** radio button, and then cick **Next**.

13. Click **Finish** to configure the server as a Distributor. SQL Server then configures your server as the Publisher, Distributor, and Subscriber. Enterprise Manager should present a notification that the Replication Monitor has been added to allow monitoring of all replication activity. Click **OK**, and then click **Close**.

14. In Enterprise Manager, click the **Tools** menu, point to **Replication**, and then click **Create and Manage Publications**. The Create and Manage Publications dialog box opens.

15. Click **Create Publication**. The Create Publication Wizard starts. Click **Next**. The Choose Publication Database screen appears.

16. Select the **Northwind** database, and then click **Next**. The Select Publication Type screen appears.

17. Click **Merge publication**, and then click **Next**. The Specify Subscriber Types screen appears.

18. Verify that the **Servers running SQL Server 2000** option is selected, and then click **Next**. The Specify Articles screen appears.

19. Verify that **Tables** is selected in the Object Type list. In the Object list box, click the **Products** table in the right scope, and then click **Next**. The Article Issues screen appears.

20. Read over the issues and the descriptions, and then click **Next**. The Select Publication Name and Description screen appears.

21. Accept the default name, and then click **Next**. The Customize the Properties and the Publication screen appears.

22. Verify that the **No, create the publication as specified** option is selected. Click **Next**. Then, click **Finish** to confirm the creation of the publication. The SQL Server Enterprise Manager dialog box opens.

23. Read the warning information, and then click **Close**. You are returned to the Create and Manage Publications dialog box.

24. Click **Push New Subscriptions**. The Create Push Subscription Wizard starts. Click **Next**. The Choose Subscribers screen appears.

25. Click your *server_name* under the Enabled Subscribers tree, and then click **Next**. The Choose Destination Database screen appears.

26. Type **pubs** in the Subscription database name text box, and then click **Next**. The Set Merge Agent Schedule screen appears.

27. Click **Continuously**, and then click **Next**. The Initialize Subscription dialog box opens.

28. Verify that the **Yes, initialize the schema and data** radio button is selected, and then click **Next**. The Set Subscription Priority screen appears.

29. Verify that the **Use the Publisher as a proxy for the Subscriber when resolving conflicts** option is selected, and then click **Next**. The Start Required Services screen appears.

30. Verify that the SQLServerAgent service is selected and running, and then click **Next**. You are returned to the Creating Push Subscription Wizard screen. Click **Finish**.

31. The SQL Server Enterprise Manager dialog box opens indicating the subscriptions were successfully created. Click **Close**. You are returned to the Create and Manage Publications dialog box.

32. Click **Close**. You are returned to Enterprise Manager.

33. Expand **Databases** and then expand **pubs**. Click **Tables**, right-click **Products**, click **Open Table**, and then click **Return all rows**. If you see records, your subscription has been successfully replicated from the Northwind database into the pubs database. Click **Close**.

34. To close Enterprise Manager, click the **Close** button in the top-right corner of the window.

35. Click **Start**, point to **Programs**, point to **Administrative Tools**, and then click **Services**. The Services window appears.

36. Right-click the **SQLSERVERAGENT** service, and click **Stop**.

37. To close the Services window, click the **Close** button in the top-right corner of the window.

Certification Objectives

Objectives for Microsoft Exam #70-228: Installing, Configuring, and Administering Microsoft SQL Server 2000 Enterprise Edition:

➤ Configure, maintain, and troubleshoot replication services

Review Questions

1. Which wizard allows you to configure the Publisher, Distributor, and Subscribers?
   a. Configure Subscriber Wizard
   b. Create Publication Wizard
   c. Configure Publishing and Distribution Wizard
   d. Create Push Subscription Wizard

2. Which wizard will push the subscription to the Subscriber?
   a. Configure Subscriber Wizard
   b. Create Publication Wizard
   c. Configure Publishing and Distribution Wizard
   d. Create Push Subscription Wizard

3. Where would you check if a problem occurred in replication?
   a. Windows Error Log
   b. Replication Monitor
   c. \WINNT\Logs\RepErrors.log
   d. Performance Monitor

4. What service must be started for replication to work?
   a. MS Search
   b. MSREPLICATION
   c. SQLSERVERAGENT
   d. MSDTC

5. What must happen before you can see the data on the Subscriber?
   a. The schema must be initialized
   b. The MSREPLICATION service must be started
   c. Space must be freed up on the Publisher
   d. SQL Server must be configured for backward compatibility

LAB 9.4 SUPPORTING XML IN MICROSOFT SQL SERVER 2000

Objectives

The goal of this lab is to learn about how SQL Server can support XML. In this lab, you'll explore some of the T-SQL syntax that ships with SQL Server 2000 to make your queries output into XML.

Materials Required

This lab will require the following:

➤ Access to a computer running Windows 2000 Server, Windows 2000 Advanced Server, or Windows 2000 Datacenter Server with SQL Server 2000 installed

Estimated completion time: **15 minutes**

Activity Background

In this lab, you'll explore an extension to T-SQL that outputs results into XML. The FOR XML AUTO clause can be appended to your SELECT statement to output the results and automatically format the results in easy-to-use XML.

Activity

1. Boot your computer and log on, if necessary.
2. Click **Start**, point to **Programs**, point to **Microsoft SQL Server**, and then click **Books Online**. The SQL Server Books Online window appears.
3. In the Navigation pane, click the **Index** tab. Type **XML** in the keyword text box, and then select the **AUTO** topic under XML.
4. This topic describes in detail the FOR XML AUTO command's syntax. Read through the information displayed.
5. To close Books Online, click the **Close** button in the top-right corner of the window.
6. Click **Start**, point to **Programs**, point to **Microsoft SQL Server**, and then click **Query Analyzer**. The SQL Server Enterprise Manager window appears.
7. Verify that **(local)** is listed in the SQL Server text box and that the **Windows authentication** radio button is selected, and then click **OK**. The SQL Query Analyzer window appears.
8. Click the **Database** list arrow, and then click **Northwind**.
9. Click the **Query** menu, and then click **Results in Text**.
10. In the query window, type the following text:

    **select Customers.CustomerID, Orders.OrderID,
    Customers.ContactName
    from Customers, Orders
    where Customers.CustomerID = Orders.CustomerID
    order by Customers.CustomerID
    for XML AUTO**

    and then execute the command by pressing **F5**. Pay special attention to the names of the XML tags in the Results pane.
11. To close Query Analyzer, click the **Close** button in the top-right corner of the window. When prompted to save the query, click **No To All**.

Review Questions

1. What would be the correct syntax to output every record in the Products table to XML?
   a. SELECT * FROM Products FOR XML ORDER BY ProductID
   b. SELECT * FROM Products ORDER BY ProductID FOR XML AUTO
   c. SELECT * FROM Products ORDER BY ProductID FOR XML AUTO OUTPUT
   d. SELECT * FROM Products FOR XML AUTO GROUP BY ProductID

2. What function is not directly supported with the FOR XML AUTO clause?
   a. ORDER BY
   b. SELECT
   c. TOP
   d. GROUP BY

3. What keyword would you use to map table columns to subelements?
   a. EXPLICIT
   b. SUBELEMENT
   c. ELEMENTS
   d. TRUE

4. Which two of the following queries would have invalid syntax?
   a. SELECT ProductID, ProductNm FROM Products WHERE ProductID = 1 FOR XML ORDER BY ProductID
   b. SELECT ProductID, ProductNm FROM Products WHERE ProductID = 1 ORDER BY ProductID FOR XML
   c. SELECT * FROM Products GROUP BY ProductID FOR XML AUTO, SUBELEMENTS
   d. SELECT * FROM Products FOR XML AUTO, ELEMENTS

5. Which of the following queries would return the XML string for the fully qualified location of a customer where a state existed?
   a. SELECT City & ',' & Region & ' ' & Country as FullRegion
      From Customers
      WHERE REGION IS NOT NULL
      FOR XML AUTO
   b. SELECT City + ',' + Region + ' ' + Country as FullRegion
      From Customers
      WHERE REGION IS NOT NULL
      FOR XML AUTO
   c. SELECT City, ',', Region, ' ', Country as FullRegion
      From Customers
      WHERE REGION IS NOT NULL
      FOR XML AUTO
   d. SELECT City + ',' + Region + ' ' + Country as FullRegion
      From Customers
      FOR XML AUTO, IGNORENULLS(Region)

CHAPTER TEN

Automating and Monitoring SQL Server 2000

Labs included in this chapter

➤ Lab 10.1 Configuring SQL Server Agent
➤ Lab 10.2 Creating Operators
➤ Lab 10.3 Creating Jobs
➤ Lab 10.4 Creating Alerts

Microsoft MCSE Exam #70-228 Objectives

Objective	Lab
Configure alerts and operators by using SQL Server Agent	10.2, 10.4
Create, manage, and troubleshoot SQL Server Agent jobs	10.3

Lab 10.1 Configuring SQL Server Agent

Objectives

The goal of this lab is to become familiar with the SQL Server Agent service. You will start the service, configure the service to start whenever the computer is restarted, view the error log, and configure the recipient of net send commands.

Materials Required

This lab will require the following:

➤ Access to a computer running Windows 2000 Server, Windows 2000 Advanced Server, or Windows 2000 Datacenter Server with SQL Server 2000 installed

➤ The SQL Server Agent service must be stopped (if previously started)

Estimated completion time: **15 minutes**

Activity Background

The SQL Server Agent is a database administrator's best friend, running routine tasks on a regular basis, and keeping tabs on important statistics about your database. These "helping hands" are facilitated with jobs, alerts, and operators, and you will get some practice creating each of these in later labs. But first, you must start and configure the service. The SQL Server Agent service is completely separate from the database engine, and stores all its information in the msdb database. Also in this lab, you will view the error log, which is helpful when confirming the completion of jobs and troubleshooting Agent activities that are not functioning properly.

Activity

1. Boot your computer, and log on by pressing **Ctrl+Alt+Del**. In the Log On to Windows window, type your user name and password in the text boxes, and then press **Enter**. The Windows 2000 desktop appears on your screen.

2. Click **Start**, point to **Programs**, point to **Microsoft SQL Server**, and then click **Enterprise Manager**. The SQL Server Enterprise Manager window appears.

3. Expand **Microsoft SQL Servers**, expand **SQL Server Group**, expand your *server_name*, and then expand **Management**.

4. Right-click **SQL Server Agent**, and then click **Properties**. The SQL Server Agent Properties dialog box opens.

5. On the General tab, under Error log, click **View**. The View SQL Server Agent Error Log dialog box opens indicating that the error log file does not exist. This is because the SQL Server Agent service has not yet started, and therefore, an error log is not yet needed.

Lab 10.1 Configuring SQL Server Agent 193

6. Click **OK**.
7. On the General tab, under Error log, click the File name browse button (**...**). The Error Log File Location dialog box opens.
8. Notice the default file name and location for the error log.
9. Click **Cancel** twice to return to Enterprise Manager.
10. In the tree pane, under the Management folder, right-click **SQL Server Agent**, and then click **Start**. The SQL Server Agent service starts, and the SQL Server Agent icon changes from a red square to a green triangle.
11. Click **Start**, point to **Programs**, point to **Administrative Tools**, and then click **Computer Management**. The Computer Management window appears.
12. Expand **Services and Applications**, and then click **Services**.
13. In the list of services displayed on the right side of the window, scroll down and double-click the **SQLSERVERAGENT** service. The SQLSERVERAGENT Properties (Local Computer) dialog box opens.
14. Click the **Startup type** list arrow, and then click **Automatic**.
15. Click **OK**.
16. To close Computer Management, click the **Close** button in the top-right corner of the window. You are returned to Enterprise Manager.
17. Right-click **SQL Server Agent**, and then click **Display Error Log**. The SQL Server Agent Error Log (Filtered) dialog box opens.
18. Click the **Type** list arrow, and then click **All Types**, as shown in Figure 10-1.

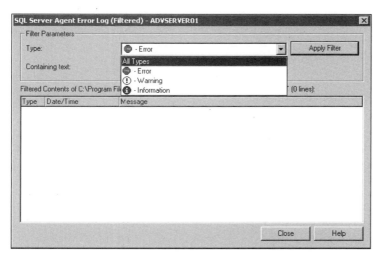

Figure 10-1 Removing the filter on the SQL Server Agent Error Log

19. Read through the informational messages and warnings, and then click **Close**.
20. Right-click **SQL Server Agent**, and then click **Properties**. The SQL Server Agent Properties dialog box opens.
21. Under Error log, notice that the option to change the file name and location is no longer available. This is due to the file being open and in use by the SQL Server Agent service. Also notice that you can view the error log from this dialog box.
22. In the Net send recipient text box, type your *server_name*.
23. Click the **Advanced** tab, and then click **Auto restart SQL Server Agent if it stops unexpectedly**.
24. Click the remaining three tabs (**Alert System**, **Job System**, and **Connection**), and read through the information/options displayed.
25. Click **OK**. The SQL Server Agent Properties dialog box opens, asking if you want to restart the SQL Server Agent service.
26. Click **Yes**. The Configure SQL Server Agent dialog box opens, indicating that the SQL Server Agent service was successfully restarted.
27. Click **OK**.
28. To close Enterprise Manager, click the **Close** button in the top-right corner of the window.

Review Questions

1. On which tab of the SQL Server Agent Properties dialog box will you find the option to include the body of e-mails in the notification page?
   a. General
   b. Advanced
   c. Alert System
   d. Job System

2. On which tab of the SQL Server Agent Properties dialog box will you find the option to change the account name and password for the SQL Server Agent service startup account?
   a. General
   b. Advanced
   c. Job System
   d. Connection

3. On which tab of the SQL Server Agent Properties dialog box will you find the option to change the SQL Server connection method (Windows or SQL Server)?
   a. Advanced
   b. Alert System
   c. Job System
   d. Connection

4. On which tab of the SQL Server Agent Properties dialog box will you find the option to change the restart policy?
   a. General
   b. Advanced
   c. Alert System
   d. Connection

5. On which tab of the SQL Server Agent Properties dialog box will you find the option to limit the size of the job history log?
   a. Advanced
   b. Alert System
   c. Job System
   d. Connection

LAB 10.2 CREATING OPERATORS

Objectives

The goal of this lab is to create two operators, one with Enterprise Manager and one with the T-SQL system stored procedure sp_add_operator.

Materials Required

This lab will require the following:

➤ Access to a computer running Windows 2000 Server, Windows 2000 Advanced Server, or Windows 2000 Datacenter Server with SQL Server 2000 installed

➤ Completion of Lab 10.1 (so that the SQL Server Agent service is started and configured to start automatically after a computer restart)

Estimated completion time: **20 minutes**

Activity Background

Before we can start automating routine tasks for our database, we must first create one or more operators. These operators can then be notified when jobs complete, where errors occur, or when a condition that you define is met.

ACTIVITY

1. Boot your computer and log on, if necessary.

2. Click **Start**, point to **Programs**, point to **Microsoft SQL Server**, and then click **Books Online**. The SQL Server Books Online window appears.

3. In the Navigation pane, click the **Search** tab. Type **"defining operators"** (including the quotes) in the search criteria text box, and then click **List Topics**. The results of the search are displayed.

4. Under Select topic, double-click **Defining Operators** in the location Administering SQL Server. Read through the information displayed.

5. Under See Also, click the **sp_add_operator** link to view the T-SQL code.

6. To close Books Online, click the **Close** button in the top-right corner of the window.

7. Click **Start**, point to **Programs**, point to **Microsoft SQL Server**, and then click **Enterprise Manager**. The SQL Server Enterprise Manager window appears.

8. Expand **Microsoft SQL Servers**, expand **SQL Server Group**, and then expand your *server_name*.

9. Expand **Management**, and then expand **SQL Server Agent**.

10. Right-click **Operators**, and then click **New Operator**. The New Operator Properties dialog box opens.

11. In the Name text box, type **22LM_Op1**.

12. In the Net send address text box, type your *server_name*, and then click **Test**. The Test Net Send Address dialog box opens, asking if it's OK to send a message to your *server_name*.

13. Click **OK**. The Messenger Service dialog box opens, displaying a test pop-up message.

14. Click **OK** twice to create the new operator.

15. Click **Start**, point to **Programs**, point to **Microsoft SQL Server**, and then click **Query Analyzer**. The Connect to SQL Server dialog box opens.

16. Verify that **(local)** is listed in the SQL Server text box, and that the **Windows authentication** radio button is selected, and then click **OK**. The SQL Query Analyzer window appears.

17. In the query window, type the following text:

    use msdb
    exec sp_add_operator @name = '228LM_Op2',
    @netsend_address = '*server_name*'
    go

    and execute the command by pressing **F5**. The message "The command(s) completed successfully." appears in the bottom section of the query window.

18. To close Query Analyzer, click the **Close** button in the top-right corner of the window. The SQL Query Analyzer dialog box opens, asking if you want to save changes.

19. Click **No To All**. You are returned to Enterprise Manager.
20. In the Tree pane, right-click **Operators**, and then click **Refresh**. The operator just created in Query Analyzer is displayed in the Operators list on the right side of the window.
21. To close Enterprise Manager, click the **Close** button in the top-right corner of the window.

Certification Objectives

Objectives for Microsoft Exam #70-228: Installing, Configuring, and Administering Microsoft SQL Server 2000 Enterprise Edition:

➤ Configure alerts and operators by using SQL Server Agent

Review Questions

1. What is required to notify an operator by e-mail?
    a. Microsoft Outlook
    b. Microsoft Exchange client
    c. Any e-mail client
    d. A MAPI-1 compliant e-mail client

2. What operating systems will support the use of net send notifications?
    a. Any Windows operating system
    b. Any Windows NT 4.0 or Windows 2000 operating system
    c. Windows NT Server or any Windows 2000 Server operating system
    d. Any Windows 2000 operating system

3. What should you do if you are notifying operators by pager, and you are using a low-capacity alphanumeric paging system?
    a. Shorten the maximum length of an operator's name to 16 characters
    b. Shorten the subject line to 16 characters
    c. Shorten the text of the message by excluding the error text from notification
    d. Restrict the use of CCs

4. Using the T-SQL system stored procedure sp_add_operator, you create a new operator and include the @pager_days = 20. What days of the week will this operator be available?
    a. Tuesday and Thursday
    b. Monday, Wednesday, and Friday
    c. Monday through Friday
    d. The first 20 days of each month

5. What database must you be in to execute the system stored procedure sp_add_operator?
   a. master
   b. model
   c. msdb
   d. Northwind

LAB 10.3 CREATING JOBS

Objectives

The goal of this lab is to create a SQL Server Agent job using the Create Job Wizard, and then manually using the New Job Properties dialog box.

Materials Required

This lab will require the following:

> Access to a computer running Windows 2000 Server, Windows 2000 Advanced Server, or Windows 2000 Datacenter Server with SQL Server 2000 installed

> Completion of Lab 10.1 (so that the SQL Server Agent service is started and configured to start automatically after a computer restart)

> The 228LM_Op1 and 228LM_Op2 operators, created in Lab 10.2

> The CompanyONE database, created in Lab 5.2

Estimated completion time: **25 minutes**

Activity Background

Now that you have configured the SQL Server Agent service and created the necessary operators, you can begin to automate tasks and prepare for possible problems. In this lab, you will create two jobs to run on a regular schedule. You will create the first job with the help of a wizard, so that you can become familiar with the type of information needed. Then you will bypass the wizard and create a job using the New Job Properties page.

ACTIVITY

To create a job using the Create Job Wizard:

1. Boot your computer and log on, if necessary.

2. Click **Start**, point to **Programs**, point to **Microsoft SQL Server**, and then click **Enterprise Manager**. The SQL Server Enterprise Manager window appears.

3. Expand **Microsoft SQL Servers**, expand **SQL Server Group**, and then expand your *server_name*.

4. Expand **Management**, and then click **SQL Server Agent**.

5. Click the **Tools** menu, and then click **Wizards**. The Select Wizard dialog box opens.

6. Expand **Management**, click **Create Job Wizard**, and then click **OK**. The Create Job Wizard starts.

7. Click **Next**. The Select job command type screen appears.

8. Verify that the **Transact-SQL command** option is chosen, and then click **Next**. The Enter Transact-SQL Statement screen appears.

9. Click the **Database name** list arrow, and then click **Northwind**.

10. In the Transact-SQL statement box, type the following text:

    dbcc dbreindex (customers)
    go

    and then click **Next**. The Specify job schedule screen appears.

 When entering T-SQL commands into the statement box, you can click the Parse button to verify the syntax of your code without actually executing the commands.

11. Under When do you want the job to run?, click **On a recurring basis**, and then click **Schedule**. The Edit Recurring Job Schedule dialog box opens.

12. Under Occurs, click **Daily**, and then change the frequency to Every **3** day(s), as shown in Figure 10-2.

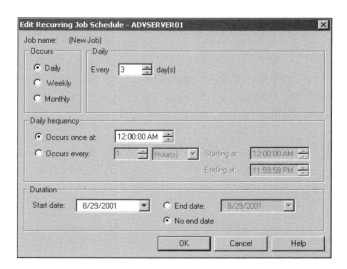

Figure 10-2 Setting a recurring job schedule

13. Accept the defaults for the Daily frequency and Duration options, and then click **OK**. You are returned to the Specify job schedule screen.
14. Click **Next**. The Job Notifications screen appears.
15. Click the **Net send** list arrow, and then click **228LM_Op1**.
16. Click **Next**. The Completing the Create Job Wizard screen appears.
17. In the Job name text box, type **ReIndex Customers**.
18. Click **Finish**. The Create Job Wizard dialog box opens indicating that the job was successfully created.
19. Click **OK**. You are returned to Enterprise Manager.
20. In the Tree pane, expand **SQL Server Agent**, and then click **Jobs**. The job just created appears in the list on the right side of the screen.

If you completed Lab 7.6, then you will see an additional four jobs relating to the AllDBMaintPlan maintenance plan. If you completed Lab 9.3, you will see an additional seven jobs relating to replication in your list.

21. Right-click **ReIndex Customers**, and then click **Properties**. The ReIndex Customers Properties dialog box opens.
22. Review the information/options on the four tabs (**General**, **Steps**, **Schedules**, and **Notifications**).
23. Click **Cancel**. If the ReIndex Customers Properties dialog box opens asking if you want to save the changes made, click **No**.

To create a backup device for the CompanyONE database (this will be necessary to complete the last part of this lab):

1. In the Tree pane, right-click **Backup**, and then click **New Backup Device**. The Backup Device Properties dialog box opens.
2. In the Name text box, type **C1Device**, and then click **OK**.

To create a job using the New Job Properties dialog box:

1. In the Tree pane, right-click **Jobs**, and then click **New Job**. The New Job Properties dialog box opens.
2. On the General tab, in the Name text box, type **Full Backup of CompanyONE**.
3. Click the **Steps** tab, and then click **New**. The New Job Step dialog box opens.
4. In the Step name text box, type **Backup Database**.
5. Verify that **Transact-SQL Script** (**TSQL**) is listed in the Type list, and **master** is listed in the Database list.

6. In the Command text box, type the following text (as shown in Figure 10-3):

   **backup database CompanyONE
   to C1Device
   go**

   and then click **OK**.

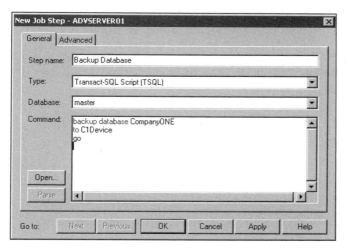

Figure 10-3 The New Job Step dialog box

7. Click the **Schedules** tab, and then click **New Schedule**. The New Job Schedule dialog box opens.

8. In the Name text box, type **Once a week**, and then verify that **Recurring** is selected, and then click **OK**.

9. Click the **Notifications** tab. Click **Net send operator**, click the **Net send operator** list arrow, and then click **228LM_Op2**.

Notice that the default for when to notify this operator is When the job fails. When creating a job using the wizard, the default is Whenever the job completes.

10. Click **OK**. The job is created and you are returned to Enterprise Manager.

11. In the list of jobs, right-click **Full Backup of CompanyONE**, and then click **Start Job**.

12. Right-click **Full Backup of CompanyONE**, and then click **View Job History**. The Job History dialog box opens.

13. Read through the information displayed, and then click **Close**.

14. To close Enterprise Manager, click the **Close** button in the top-right corner of the window.

Certification Objectives

Objectives for Microsoft Exam #70-228: Installing, Configuring, and Administering Microsoft SQL Server 2000 Enterprise Edition:

➤ Create, manage, and troubleshoot SQL Server Agent jobs

Review Questions

1. On which tab of a Job Properties dialog box will you find the option to create a new alert?
    a. General
    b. Steps
    c. Schedules
    d. Notifications

2. On which tab of a Job Properties dialog box will you find the option to disable a job?
    a. General
    b. Steps
    c. Schedules
    d. Notifications

3. On which tab of a Job Properties dialog box will you find the option to automatically delete a job when it succeeds, fails, or completes?
    a. General
    b. Steps
    c. Schedules
    d. Notifications

4. On which tab of a Job Properties dialog box will you find the option to create or edit a description for a job?
    a. General
    b. Steps
    c. Schedules
    d. Notifications

5. On which tab of a Job Properties dialog box will you find the option to rearrange the order of the steps in a job?
    a. General
    b. Steps
    c. Schedules
    d. Notifications

LAB 10.4 CREATING ALERTS

Objectives

The goal of this lab is to create an event alert and a performance condition alert, one with and one without the use of the Create Alert Wizard.

Materials Required

This lab will require the following:

- Access to a computer running Windows 2000 Server, Windows 2000 Advanced Server, or Windows 2000 Datacenter Server with SQL Server 2000 installed
- Completion of Lab 10.1 (so that the SQL Server Agent service is started and configured to start automatically after a computer restart)
- The 228LM_Op2 operator, created in Lab 10.2
- The CompanyONE database, created in Lab 5.2
- Completion of Lab 10.3 (so that the CompanyONE database has been backed up to the C1Device)

Estimated completion time: **30 minutes**

Activity Background

Database administrators are very busy people, and it would be impossible to continually monitor your server and all the databases on it manually. The SQL Server Agent will do this for you automatically, if you indicate what to watch. Alerts come in two flavors—event alerts and performance condition alerts. Event alerts are fired based on an error number or severity level. Performance condition alerts are fired when a counter falls below, becomes equal to, or rises above a value that you set. When either type of alert fires, the SQL Server Agent can respond to the alert by executing a job, notifying an operator, or both.

Activity

To create an event alert using the Create Alert Wizard:

1. Boot your computer and log on, if necessary.
2. Click **Start**, point to **Programs**, point to **Microsoft SQL Server**, and then click **Books Online**. The SQL Server Books Online window appears.
3. In the Navigation pane, click the **Search** tab. Type **"defining alerts"** (including the quotes) in the search criteria text box, and then click **List Topics**. The results of the search are displayed.
4. Under Select topic, double-click **Defining Alerts** in the location Administering SQL Server. Read through the information displayed.

Chapter 10   Automating and Monitoring SQL Server 2000

5. To close Books Online, click the **Close** button in the top-right corner of the window.

6. Click **Start**, point to **Programs**, point to **Microsoft SQL Server**, and then click **Enterprise Manager**. The SQL Server Enterprise Manager window appears.

7. Expand Microsoft **SQL Servers**, expand **SQL Server Group**, and then expand your *server_name*.

8. Expand **Management**, expand **SQL Server Agent**, and then click **Alerts**.

9. Click the **Tools** menu, and then click **Wizards**. The Select Wizard dialog box opens.

10. Expand **Management**, click **Create Alert Wizard**, and then click **OK**. The Create Alert Wizard starts.

11. Click **Next**. The Define the Alert screen appears.

12. Under Raise this alert, click **Only if this error occurs**, type **9002** in the text box, and then click **Next**. The Specify a Database or Error Keywords screen appears.

13. Click the **Database name** list arrow, click **CompanyONE**, and then click **Next**. The Define Alert Response screen appears.

14. Click the **Job to execute** list arrow, and then click **(New Job)**, as shown in Figure 10-4. The New Job Properties dialog box opens.

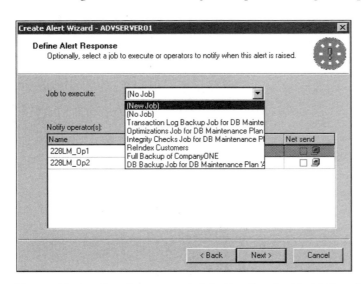

Figure 10-4   Creating a new job in the Create Alert Wizard

15. On the General tab, in the Name text box, type **T-Log Backup of CompanyONE**.

16. Click the **Steps** tab, and then click **New**. The New Job Step dialog box opens.

17. In the Step name text box, type **Backup Log**.

18. Verify that **Transact-SQL Script (TSQL)** is listed in the Type list, and **master** is listed in the Database list.

19. In the Command text box, type the following text:

    **backup log CompanyONE
    to C1Device
    go**

    and then click **OK**. You are returned to the New Job Properties dialog box.

20. Click **OK**. You are returned to the Define Alert Response screen.

21. Under Notify operator(s), click the **Net send** box for 228LM_Op2, and then click **Next**. The Define Alert Notification Message screen appears.

22. In the Include error message text in section, click to uncheck E-mail, as shown in Figure 10-5.

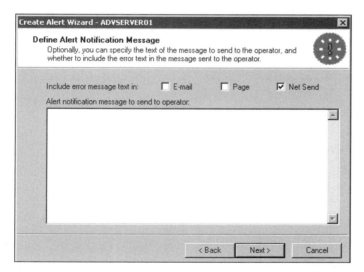

Figure 10-5 Defining the alert notification message

23. Click **Next**. The Completing the Create Alert Wizard starts.

24. In the Alert name text box, type **C1 T-Log full**, and then click **Finish**.
    The Create Alert Wizard dialog box opens indicating that the alert was successfully created.

25. Click **OK**. You are returned to Enterprise Manager.

To create a performance alert using the New Alert Properties dialog box:

1. In the Tree pane, right-click **Alerts**, and then click **New Alert**. The New Alert Properties dialog box opens.

2. On the General tab, in the Name text box, type **C1 T-Log 80% full**.

3. Click the **Type** list arrow, and then click **SQL Server performance condition alert**.

4. Under Performance condition alert definition, click the **Object** list arrow, and then click **SQL Server:Databases**.

5. Click the **Counter** list arrow, and then click **Percent Log Used**.

6. Click the **Instance** list arrow, and then click **CompanyONE**.

7. Click the **Alert if counter** list arrow, and then click **rises above**, and then type **80** in the Value text box, as shown in Figure 10-6.

Figure 10-6 The General tab of the New Alert Properties dialog box

8. Click the **Response** tab.

9. Click to select the **Execute job** check box, click the **Execute job** list arrow, and then click **T-Log Backup of CompanyONE** (if necessary).

10. Under Operators to notify, click the **Net Send** box for 228LM_Op2.

11. For Include alert error text in, click to uncheck **E-mail**, as shown in Figure 10-7.

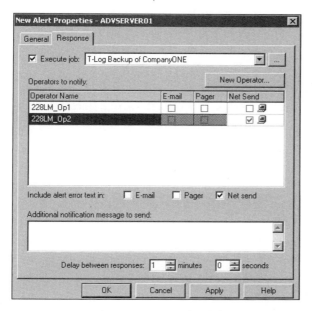

Figure 10-7 The Response tab of the New Alert Properties dialog box

12. Click **OK**. The alert is created and you are returned to Enterprise Manager.

Certification Objectives

Objectives for Microsoft Exam #70-228: Installing, Configuring, and Administering Microsoft SQL Server 2000 Enterprise Edition:

➤ Configure alerts and operators by using SQL Server Agent

Review Questions

1. Where are events that are automatically generated by Microsoft SQL Server entered?
   a. The SQL Server events log
   b. Microsoft Windows Application Log
   c. Microsoft Windows Security Log
   d. Microsoft Windows System Log

2. SQL Server events of what severity level or higher are logged automatically?
   a. 39
   b. 29
   c. 19
   d. 9

3. What system stored procedure is used to designate specific errors as "always logged"?
   a. sp_altermessage
   b. sp_altererror
   c. sp_alterlog
   d. sp_alteralwayslogged

4. What database must you be in to execute the sp_add_alert system stored procedure?
   a. master
   b. model
   c. msdb
   d. tempdb

5. Which of the following will add a notification to an alert named Alert1 for an operator named Operator1 to be notified by a net send message?
   a. sp_add_notification 'Alert1', 'Operator1', 1
   b. sp_add_notification 'Alert1', 'Operator1', 2
   c. sp_add_notification 'Alert1', 'Operator1', 3
   d. sp_add_notification 'Alert1', 'Operator1', 4